GRIEF
MATTERS

Janice M. Mann

Published by Serenity Publishing

Printed by Createspace

Available from Amazon.com,
JaniceMann.com
Createspace.com and
other online stores.

ISBN - 13:9781516865369

ISBN - 10:1516865367

DEDICATION

This book is dedicated to all those spiritual
beings having a human experience that I
have met, created relationships with,
journeyed along beside, loved, lost,
forgiven, loved more, and earned incredibly
powerful lessons alongside. You know who
you are!

TABLE OF CONTENTS

INTRODUCTION

I have been waiting for you to show up. It is time for you to have this information at your fingertips. You are meant to have picked this book up to read at this moment in your life. It has been my life experience that when the student is ready the teacher appears.

There is no such thing as a coincidence. Everything in the Universe happens for a reason. We don't always know why or understand why an event happens. We have the opportunity to learn more about ourselves and others while we attempt to figure out why and how events transpire. The Universe is in complete control of everything even if it seems to you that it is not. We are exactly where we need to be. Yes, even when we are heartbroken and grieving! The solution is to ask your Inner Intelligence, the Holy Spirit Within, your

Higher Power, also known as God for insight and wisdom. Have patience!

An answer will come if we quiet our minds and listen.

I have written this book from the mindset that you are my dear friend. I want you to trust that I know what I am talking about. I am going to walk with you through one of the most incredible, life changing experiences in which you will participate. I have had numerous family losses, work losses, pet losses and breakups of significant relationships. I have fought severe physical illnesses. I have known the feeling of loss quite often. I have learned to make grief my friend. I know that sounds ridiculous to some of you. Grief a friend? Hardly! Perhaps an enemy! I have found over time that once I see the gifts of grief in my life it can take on another energy. An energy of gratitude for what I have shared, who I have had the opportunity to have loved and how blessed I am for the experience. Without grief we cannot experience joy, excitement or happiness! You are on your own personal journey in life. There will be moments of joy. There will be moments of pain. That is just the way it works.

How you handle the pain will make a huge difference in how you perceive the joys in life. Your highest highs in life will be equal to your lowest lows in life. It is how this journey works. Grief matters. How you experience your grief will indicate how you accept what is in your life. No one is promised a life without pain. There is no such thing as fair. Anyone who taught you the concept that life is fair lied to you. However, life is precious, sacred and far too short to hold on to resentments. Take a deep breath. Relax. Let me help you see differently. Transform your mind with knowledge. Free yourself of old thoughts and patterns. Open your mind to seeing differently.

WARNING: Reading this book may cause the quality of your life to change for the better forever! Your consciousness may be raised with some surrender, acceptance and grace!

ACKNOWLEDGEMENTS

Grief is an all-encompassing state of being. No one book can possibly address all the forms of grief.

This book is addressing the grief process due to the death of a loved one. I have chosen not to address and include other grief topics in this book. The most important components of this book are in teaching you, the reader, how to understand the process and learn how to make grief your friend.

Special thanks to Allison Strange for illustrating the front and back covers of the book.

Special thanks to Agnes M. Wilson II for editing this book.

Special thanks to Hali Confer, Debra Cutler, Patricia Gyulay, Karen Hanner, Des Jackson, Wanda James, Barbara King, Andrea Pawlisz, Lisa Snyder, Victoria Scott, Kelly Watson, Alica Williams, Agnes Wilson, Tina Zeff, Debra Zimmerman for your help with the grief research.

Rest In Peace Barak Asher

Janice M. Mann is available for public speaking engagements and private consultations. You may contact her office at Jan@JaniceMann.com.

A collection of Grief Cards written by Janice M. Mann are available for sale at www.JaniceMann.com in the store.

CHAPTER ONE

WHAT IS GRIEF?

I believe that you are reading this book at this specific moment because you or someone you love are experiencing feeling heartbroken. Heartbreak and grief go hand in hand. Grief is a natural part of the life cycle. It is a painful experience for most.

First, let me share with you a very important Universal Law: **Love Never Dies!**

Let's look at these three questions first.

What is grief?

Where does it come from?

Where does it go when it leaves?

Grief has many names including mourning, bereavement, heartache, anguish, sorrow and heartbreak.   I define it as a natural response and an individual process to a loss or a perceived loss of someone or something that we are attached and emotionally invested in having in our life as in a relationship, a death, a loss of a job or promotion at work, the death of a beloved pet, the reality of divorce and the loss of our dreams. Grief and loss are our responses to the natural rhythms of the circle of life. Sometimes it is a devastating and tortured feeling caused by the change or end of a familiar pattern of behavior. Familiar natural patterns of behavior bring us a sense of comfort and safety. In grief, one sees sadness everywhere. Grief colors your entire vision of existence. Part of the grief syndrome of loss is the sense of inability to replace what was lost or what it symbolized. It is as if the loss of a loved one is equal to the loss of love itself.

Grief comes from your soul. The price of loving someone is the grief you feel when you are no longer connected on this physical plane. It manifests itself in your physical body and energetic fields. You may experience a feeling of tightening in your throat, an empty feeling in your Solar Plexus Chakra - Stomach area, lack of energy to do the slightest thing, a pattern of sighing repeatedly, choking or shortness of, breath and distress described as stressed out or inner tension.

Common in grief is a connectedness to psychosomatic disorders, high blood pressure, vomiting/nausea, colitis, and the likelihood that other issues may be triggered. Grief may trigger medical and psychiatric issues for those who have bi-polar disorder, schizophrenia, addiction, depression and other illnesses. Pay attention to how you are feeling. Keep a journal with your thoughts, feelings, fears and the date so you can review it throughout your experience

Grief is inherent within us; just as joy, happiness, comfort and contentment are built in us. We arrived on this Earth with certain built in mechanisms and gifts. Grief is an energy that is heavy laden and sluggish.

Major losses in early life make one vulnerable to the passive acceptance of grief, as though sorrow is the price of life.

The degree of your grief is based on these factors: the emotional closeness of the deceased, the method of dying, the age at death, your Spiritual Beliefs and Your Wounded Self.

When grief leaves us it goes back into the ethers that it came from. Let me be very clear here. You most likely will always have some level of residual grief that stays with you day after day and year after year. It will not be a high sustaining level of pain for forever. I still grieve the loss of my mother after twelve years of her passing. I would not want her to come back even though I know she is out of physical pain and hanging out with the angels on the Other Side. She was fragile and ill. It was her time to go. She had fought the good fight. That didn't mean I was immune to heartbreak though. It means that I loved her enough to support her in her passing. I accepted what was inevitable. I choose to be grateful for all the time and memories we have had together. I acknowledge that I miss her presence on this physical plane daily.

Heartbreak is an emotional, physical and spiritual event when it happens. You actually feel the physical ache in your heart area. We call the area the Heart Chakra in Eastern Thought. The ache does not go away by willing it away. It stays as an unwelcome visitor in your life until you find the strength to move through the pain. You will find the strength in time. You may have nausea or digestive issues as well. At any moment you may have constipation or diarrhea. They go together. Fluttering feelings in the stomach are often reported. The energy of grief taps into all your chakras. Your core areas of the Solar Plexus Chakra, Throat Chakra and the Heart Chakra experience a mighty jolt. Don't be surprised if headaches, neck aches or back aches appear. They show up after your body has tensed up physically for quite some time.

Some folks find that they have been grinding their teeth and clenching their jaws. Our grief manifests itself into our muscular system. Every part of your body system has the opportunity to respond to the emotional and spiritual pain you are feeling in your body.

We are energy. Energy moves and changes Every second. Grief moves and changes every second. You may feel guilt, rage, anger, sorrow.

You may have uncontrollable laughter rather than uncontrollable tears. Laughter is an emotional release. Some folks feel safer laughing than crying. Do not judge yourself. Let it come out. Let it be. Guilt shows up with the "shoulds". A mother might say "I should not have let her drive the car." A family member might say "I should not have asked him to pick me up." I should not have _____ fill in the blank. Do not should on yourself. Things happen for a reason. You do not have the power you might think you have.

Survivors Guilt is a tough dynamic to take on. After the 911 attacks on the United States there were tens of thousands of folks who experienced survivor's guilt. In Towers

One and Two there was such traumatic death. One minute they were in their offices with their office staff. Some left after the first tower was hit. Some workers stayed or came back to their offices after the Port Authority said it was okay to go back in the buildings. Tower Two was hit.

A select few thousand got out of the building. The elevator worked for a short time. Then the buildings collapsed. Survivors wondered "how did I make it out alive and he or she didn't?"

The guilt often turned to chronic depression. Others were moved to joy and gratitude.

Rage is often part of the grief response. Someone has been taken from us. We are not happy about it. We get mad at whatever symbolizes for us the Divine. Getting mad at your understanding of God is a regular response. "Why did God take him? I need him!" This is where the "It is not fair" complaints start by the way. Someone has to be blamed for the personal disaster event. This is the why-me stage. Your loved one gets blamed for not taking care of himself. Doctors get blamed for not doing enough. Funeral Directors get blamed for taking too much money and not making the loved one look more lifelike. I cannot tell you how many times I have been to awake and viewing where folks would say in a whisper sound "he does not look like himself at all".

They didn't do a good job with the body ", or "the hair or the makeup or the clothes." Seriously, you can only work with what you have got!

Heartache and grief are devastating. It hits on all levels. Sometimes the pain hits all at once.

Sometimes the pain has an intermittent pattern. It can be both as well. You go from fear and anxiety to panic attacks. Simultaneously, you either cannot sleep at all or all you can do is sleep. Quite a few of us will want to self-medicate to attempt to numb the pain.   Here is an important fact to learn: **You have got to feel the pain and move through the pain to get to the other side of the pain.**

Alcohol is a depressant by its very nature. Pay attention to your level of drinking alcohol to numb your pain. The same goes with drugs other than alcohol. They may be a temporary solution for a permanent problem. Once the buzz wears off you are weary, wounded and wondering what to do next. I know. I have been there. Additionally, your thinking is fuzzy.

Stinking thinking will not serve you in the grief process. You need a clear mind to learn how to use the information your body, mind and spirit are sharing with you.

Another challenge with grief is that you cannot hold any food down or all you can do is eat comfort food. Carbohydrates and sugars are the American way with or without grief. Wherever you live you may find that when someone dies the neighbors and or the local church people bring food to the home to pay respect and save the family from cooking. It is a smorgasbord of carbohydrates and sugars. Mashed potatoes, scalloped potatoes, casseroles, pasta salads, cakes, pies, fresh hot rolls, homemade cookies and anything sweet they can think to share. You see, those compassionate friends know that sooner or later you need to eat. In America, we stuff our feeling with food quite often. Pay attention to how you grieve. The more you learn about yourself and your grieving process the better off you will be the next time grief knocks on your door. It is important to know yourself well. Grief is heartbreaking. Self-medicating with food is challenging as well. Eating feels good to some folks.

Those people who can't eat struggle too. Once you move through your grief you may need to move to the next size up or a couple of sizes down in your jeans. Be careful. Be gentle with yourself. A couple of homemade cinnamon rolls are great; but, a half dozen may be way too many! Beware of spicy foods and greasy foods. No need to add to the nausea. You will know when you are feeling up to eating those again. Watch your sugar consumption. You are going to have plenty of mood swings without adding fuel to the fire! White refined sugar is a mood swing all on its own.

In heartbreak, fatigue can be so deep you can hardly talk yourself into moving sometimes. It is a momentous occasion if you can get yourself into the shower some days. Time is a concept that has very little influence on your life when grieving.

Moments become minutes that become hours. Days seem much longer than ever before. Time does not fly. It stands still.

Don't be surprised if you lack motivation. The Life-force energy in your own being has taken a huge hit. That is one of the realities of grief.

Spiritually there are two extremes that most folks go through. The extremes are either you go to your religious and or spiritual beliefs to sustain you or you fight with the God of your understanding. It is not unusual to challenge your old beliefs and tenets.

I remember when I was with my extended family in New Jersey after 911. The husband of my sister in-law was murdered by the terrorists when the plane hit in Tower Two. Needless to say the devastation was incredulous. It was hard to observe let alone feel. My seventy five and eighty year old in-laws were Irish Catholics. They struggled with their belief that God would allow this to happen to a member of their family after they had been active church members for years, tithing and sharing. I noted that somehow, somewhere in their thinking they had created a vending store God. It appeared that they believed if they tithed to the church, went to Mass and followed the tenets of their beliefs they would be saved from this level of calamity. I felt for them as they picked up the pieces of their now broken belief system and moved forward. I honor them and their processes.

My partner at the time was devastated as well. Her sacred space was within and was made in part with lots of green plants, incredible colorful vast arrays of flowers of every kind and plenty of energy and love. Her grief took her to a place where her sacred space was no longer alive.   It was now a parched desert of arid humid heaviness. Nothing grew there. It was years before she was able to really begin anew with life. Grief has a very low heavy energy to it. It is the nature of grief to respond that way.

Grief matters. How we experience it is different for each person. We will have our own unique way of experiencing it. There is no one way to grieve.   There is no time period for grieving.   What may work for some folks may not work for others. Remove yourself from anyone if they feed you that toxic thinking. They will suck the lifeblood right out of you. Surround yourself with loving, supportive friends and family.   If the toxic thinking folks are your friends and family find a grief support group or hospice facility support group. Do not isolate yourself.

Create a safe supporting environment for yourself.

Grief is your friend.   What a crazy thought that is for many folks!   Many people see grief and emotional pain as the enemy. This is just not true.

The changes happen internally once you understand that grief is a process of acknowledging an investment in an idea or in a relationship with someone or something. I have worked and moved through incredible amounts of grief in this lifetime and worked with thousands of folks who have been dealing with their own grief process. I found that making grief my friend made it easier to accept the process. Grief has shown me many truths about myself. It told me who I loved and what I valued and treasured. It helped show me what my core beliefs are and how invested I have been in those beliefs. Look deep within while in your grief process.

You will find information about who you are. This is a gift.

GRIEF IS A PROCESS

Grief doesn't go away overnight. It decreases day by day when you have successfully emotionally, spiritually and physically moved through it. You cannot will it away. You cannot ignore it.

You can shove it down and attempt to compartmentalize it; but it will show up in another form within you over time. Sometimes it manifests itself as heart attacks, ulcers, strokes, abdominal challenges, depression and anger outbursts.

It has to be moved through your body, mind and spirit. It will happen over time in your own personal timeframe. Other people will attempt to tell you how to get over it and how long is long enough to move through it. Do not listen to them. It is on your time table. Please note that if you have not moved through your grief signs of depression may manifest and you will need to see a professional for treatment.

GRIEF HAS A NATURAL RHYTHM WITHIN YOU

Once you quit fighting to resist it and allow it to move through you it dissipates. That does not mean you are going to go through grief without feeling its effects. It has been said that once you face your fears they fade away. Facing your fears is a component of grief.

There exists a natural rhythm within you that helps facilitates healing. You will move through various stages. Trust the process.

GRIEF RESPONSES DO NOT MEAN YOU ARE CRAZY

A common feeling of people in deep grief is the feeling of going crazy. Your emotions are intense, strong and deep. You might think you are the only one to feel like this.

You are not crazy. If you reach out to others you will find you are not alone. This is a normal response.   In reality, you are very much in reality. In my experiences in life it felt very scary when I felt overwhelmed or out of control.   There is a time period where it feels that the grief is in control and we are not. When this physical, emotional and spiritual response presents itself you can truly feel out of control.   Tears come and go intermittently.   Sobbing and physically feeling the pain feels overwhelming.   It is not the sign of someone who   is feeling crazy. It will stop in time. We are not used to feeling our feelings in this culture. We invest plenty of time in self-medicating our pain with alcohol, drugs, sex, food, work, gambling, etc. It is not comfortable to grieve until you have learned how to grieve.

EMOTIONAL TRIGGERS ARE EVERYWHERE

I remember walking in a store about one year after a relationship had ended when they were young and being triggered by Easter candy. I missed the fun and the time with the children I had the opportunity to help raise in my relationship. We colored eggs each Easter and had Easter baskets full of treats when they were young. The memory of our beloved time together triggered the loss of the future of those events. I stood in the store weeping profusely. Grief had showed up without warning. I felt my feelings and allowed them to move through me. Then I chose to allow those feelings to move on and leave me.

GRIEF SHOWS UP WITHOUT WARNING

One of the more tricky dynamics of grief is that it shows up wherever whenever without warning.

The loss of someone you have loved doesn't go away with their death. It is just beginning then. I remember after my Mother passed on to the Other Side how hard it was when I had some good news and started to pick up the phone to call and share it with her. Then reality hit. She was no longer available by phone. Then emptiness and loneliness showed up. I felt like a motherless child. Grief shows up and we ache. Heartache is real. We have to sit with it. Sit with the pain. Sit with the loss. Allow it to be. Allow ourselves to be.

THERE IS NO TIME LIMIT ON GRIEVING

You are going to grieve until you have worked through your pain. This is going to depend upon numerous variables, including but not limited to, the type of grieving and the depth of your emotional investment in the relationship or situation. Do not let anyone tell you when you are supposed to be done grieving. It is not their right to tell you how to grieve. It is your right to feel your way through. It has been said that unexpected deaths of loved ones are harder on their families than when you know your loved one is terminal. I don't agree with that theory. There are different types of grief and grieving.

TELLING YOUR STORY TO WHOMEVER WILL LISTEN

You are grieving. It is unexpected and unfamiliar pain.   It is a part of your life experience and journey.   Part of this process is telling your story repeatedly to others.   I spent significant time with the 911 families after the terrorist attack in 2001. One of the first things I noticed is that each person that I shared time with had to tell me their life experience.   Repeatedly, the details of their loss were told. They shared the details of where they were when they first heard the news, who they were with, where their loved one was in the buildings, the timeline of the events, the last time they spoke with their loved ones and what was said.

They shared calling the hospitals, offices, emergency services, ministers and family.   . They told me of how much pain they were in, the fear, the terror, their children's worries, their worries about their children, how their perception of the God of their understanding played a part or did not play a part in their lives.

Each time it was shared the load of the pain got a little less. Often they didn't even realize that they were repeating themselves. It is part of the process. Each time they shared their information with anyone, it helped them ground into the reality of the hell they were living through. Change is not easy until it is. It is all in how we experience it and see it.

UNRESOLVED GRIEF IS CUMULATIVE.

Once you start grieving a specific situation or loss of a loved one any other old grief not resolved comes back to be resolved simultaneously. Don't be surprised to feel

anger, resentment, betrayal and loss over something that could be a wound from childhood.   Once our energetic system is affected by grief whatever feelings that have not been processed show up again!   You may find yourself grieving at first about your current loss.

Then you will feel the losses that have not been processed coming along so that you start feeling sad about lots of things, events or people no longer in your life.

You have given your heart deeply and completely to another being who is now physically lost to you. You have a right to mourn. You need to mourn. You need support and acceptance as you grieve.

Your heart may be in great pain now. Your heart may be in pain as deeply as you have loved.

There is no need to remain in pain as an on-going testament of your love

CHAPTER TWO

THE SYMPTOMS OF GRIEF

There are many different symptoms of grief. You may feel all of them. You may feel some of them. You will feel deeply on those you experience. These are in no specific order.

A SENSE OF LOSS OF GROUNDEDNESS

Once we have been told that someone has died or that we have had a perceived loss it is not surprising for time to temporarily stand still. It feels like we have gone into a slow motion surreal moment. The sense of not being grounded manifests. We feel as if we are floating through the day not quite connected to the ground below. It is as if someone or something has kicked our legs out from underneath us. We feel like we can't get a grip to feel grounded. This is usually brought on from the shock you feel when told of the death, anxiety and panic from the news of the loss and the reality that we are not in control.

INSOMNIA

Previously I shared with you that during grief you either cannot sleep or all you can do is sleep.   Don't be surprised if you cannot sleep.   Your world has been rocked.   The familiarity of your life just went into a tailspin. The familiarity of your comfort zone has been attacked.   It is normal to feel anxious to some degree.   You find yourself sitting up at night watching television and old movies that bring on a feeling of comfort.   Any distraction from the pain appears welcome to varying extents depending on your personality style.   There is an element of isolation as well in insomnia. You can be up all night and not have to deal with active communication with others. Up all night and sleep all day gives you less time talking with others.

ANXIETY

Anxiety happens when you forget who your Source is and fear takes hold of your thinking. Fear equals false evidence appearing real. The unfamiliar has happened. The disruption of your life by the unwelcome event is emotionally intrusive.

The unwelcomed visitor named death has come to visit.   It may bring about anxiety at the forced readjustment of your life.

We feel much more comfortable when we know the comfortable processes of life. Anxiety is a way of burning up your energy with fear and worry. When we are in a mindset of fear based thinking we are off the charts and not in the "be here now" in this moment thinking processes. Remember that faith and fear cannot exist at the same time. Put more energy in positive energy and faith based thinking.

Anxiety is a scary place to visit and a hell to live in. You feel out of control. You tell yourself thoughts based in fear. Your body and mind appear to betray you. Symptoms of anxiety include: irritability, racing thoughts, sweaty palms, lightheadedness, nausea, heart racing, and fear of heart attack and the fight or flight responses. You know that something is wrong. You don't know what it is that is wrong nor how to fix it. Most folks have an anxiety attack about having an anxiety attack. You can talk yourself into one easily. You have the power within you to talk yourself out of an anxiety attack. It is all about choosing the positive thought and believing in yourself.

Medication does not cure anxiety disorder. However, it can help you get calm so you can work through your thinking and find a new way of seeing things. You do not have to live in fear!

DEPRESSION

Depression is not grief. Grief is not depression. Depression can manifest after a period of time if you do not actively allow your grief process to happen. Depression is usually a neurological chemical imbalance in the brain. It can be situational. Most often though it is the grief process not depression. Go immediately to the local emergency room of your local hospital and ask for help if you are in such pain that you feel like you are suicidal or homicidal. Do not play with this dynamic. Seek medical attention including consideration of anti-depression and or anti-anxiety meds and review your local resources for a good therapist or grief support group. See if there exists a hospice in your area. They often offer free group grief work. Some of us just cannot handle the level of pain that can happen with grief. There are times when medication is needed. Do not feel ashamed that you need help. We all are in this journey of life together.

Each of us is uniquely different and have special needs.

FATIGUE AND EXHAUSTION

Physical, emotional and spiritual exhaustion and fatigue have the same results and it is not just being tired. Fatigue is an experience whereby you cannot think clearly, you cannot motivate yourself to get up and go and your intention is less than driven. Your get up and go got up and went! It permeates a very low level of energy. You may feel sluggish, weary and worn. Fatigue is a mental state of being while grieving. **What you are experiencing is energetic depletion**. This may frighten you as the only other times you have felt anything similar is when you are physically sick.

It is all right to be exhausted and to rest. Take time to heal. Do not push yourself. Trust your body and mind to do what they are programmed to do. Know that this is your body coping with tragic loss. The best thing you can do when grieving is allow yourself to sleep.   The challenge when sleeping is that you can be in a place where life is good again and your loved one is still alive in your dreams.   Then you wake up and the harsh reality returns repeatedly. Slowly begin to find choices that are self-loving. Choose to eat better nutrition filled meals.   Take a short walk.   Pets are a true gift when you are grieving.   Add some supplements to your diet.   Go to a movie. Write in your journal. Plant some flowers.

PANIC ATTACKS

Panic attacks show up when we have irrational fears about a specific situation. There may be no real threat.   A perceived threat is as intense as a real threat if we believe it is. Symptoms of panic attacks include, but are not limited to, sweaty palms, heart palpitations, fear you are having a heart attack, fear you are dying, a feeling of being out of control, racing thoughts, challenges in breathing and a desire to run away also known as fight or flight. The "what if's" begin to take its toll on you. We make up stories in our head about how terrible things are and how bad they are going to be. It is irrational fear based thinking. We stress ourselves out so much worrying about an oncoming panic attack that we cause a panic attack about having a panic attack. Pay attention to what your triggers are when this happens. A trigger is defined as an event or a thought that evokes a panic response.

NAUSEA

This symptom is a tough one. I don't know about you but when I am nauseous it is not pretty. You usually don't want to go anywhere too far away from a bathroom. You never know which end is going to need the facilities first. Perhaps you may not want to go out of your home at all. Your stomach is telling you something is not right. Something is NOT RIGHT. You are heartbroken. You cannot eat. The idea of eating makes you as sick as the reality of eating. Queasy is a state of being.

Your energy is spent trying to maintain a balance that is questionable at best. Many folks just want to stay in bed and not face the world for a while.

I encourage you to learn to like the finer but simpler things in life such as tea. A cup of chamomile tea, peppermint or spearmint tea can do wonders for your digestive system. Do not use fake sweetener though as it has within its ingredients other substances that will attack your digestive system. Go talk with your local pharmacist and find an over the counter anti-diarrhea medicine to help you. Do not eat milk products until your body is re-regulating itself. Milk can cause more digestive issues.

NIGHTMARES

Nightmares and night terrors are horrendously challenging dreams that have gone bad. Most always they tell us we feel out of control. They tell us that some fear and some situation is overwhelming us. If you have recently experienced a significant loss you may have nightmares or night terrors until you get more of a balanced emotional state. In reality, waking up to the harsh realities of loss is a nightmare in both the night time and the daytime for some people. We are not in control of our dream state. I have personally experienced these symptoms and have found that if I drank some calming chamomile tea it helped me rest better. It has been my experience that when nightmares have happened, it is good to turn a light on in the room, catch your breath and tell yourself you are safe. Get up and walk around so that you become more grounded in yourself rather than in your dream state. You may want to have a notebook and pen by the bed so you can write about your feelings and thoughts. However, if it had been very traumatic do not try to write about it as it may bring back your fear thoughts. You may wish to put some music on that you love that helps you to relax.

WEIGHT LOSS OR GAIN

People are unique and each of us have our vulnerabilities. Those of you that are inclined to use food as a comfort will overeat while grieving. This will bring weight gain. It is simple common sense. Eating white sugar desserts, tasty carbohydrates and chocolates will yield weight gain. Who doesn't love chocolate? Consider that when grieving we have less energy to spend and are more likely to do less physical activity it clearly sets us up to gain weight.

Weight loss is another symptom when grieving. You can't eat much when grieving. You are nauseous and queasy. You are pacing the floors with insomnia. This burns energy and without the appropriate fuel your body needs to sustain yourself causes weight loss. It is vital to make sure you eat something every three hours or so every day. It does not have to be a big meal. A piece of fresh fruit, a protein shake, and some fresh veggies are all reasonable choices. Soups are good food as well. The famous peanut butter and jelly sandwich is a good option too!

INTERMITTENT CRYING

You are going to cry, wail, sob and moan. You may find yourself screaming into a pillow or not! This may not happen around others. It may be with a few close friends. It may be when you are alone. Many folks say they want to cry and cannot. Ultimately they do cry in their time. Then the waves of grief subside and you start to feel like you might have a handle on your emotions. Just when you think you are feeling composed here come those tears again. Allow the tears to come. Go ahead and buy some tissues and keep them with you because you are going to need them. Every tear that is cried makes room for joy and happiness to come back in your life. It may feel like you have been cried out. It may feel like there cannot possibly be any more tears. I assure you that there will be more tears or laughter when needed for emotion release. Our bodies are built this way.

OVERSPENDING

Those of us that are not working within to heal ourselves will find shopping a temptation. It is a temporary solution to a permanent challenge. There is truly no way to feel better in the grief process without working through it by yourself or with others. Some people say that they get a good feeling when they go shopping. It is an external reward that may give you a sated feeling. It goes away quickly. More money has to be spent and then more and more.

The overspending becomes painful to the wallet and to your well-being. It can cause conflicts with your significant other over finances and cause additional stress to your life. It is a vicious circle if you keep using it to feel better.

LACK OF LIBIDO

Do not be surprised if you temporarily have a decline in your sex life. It is temporary. Grief takes away the urge to merge for many individuals. Lack of libido is a normal response while grieving. Exhaustion and fatigue along with a great sense of loss are just not foreplay. You must be patient with your partner if he or she is grieving someone's passing. Give them time. Give yourself time. Grief often gets in the way of sexual desire, interest and sex in general. It's common to feel uninterested in sex or have difficulty getting and/or keeping an erection. It may even feel uncomfortable taking your clothes off in front of your partner.

Clothes are the last refuge of those who feel utterly vulnerable.   Recovering intimacy and sexual pleasure following heartbreak and loss takes time. It also takes a willingness to deal with your grief before expecting too much from your physical body or sexual performance. I suggest that you communicate with your partner about these issues openly and without placing blame on anyone. Give yourself time.

HIPER SEXUAL BEHAVIOR

Everyone does not react nor respond in the same manner when in grief. Some folks will not want to have sex for some time. Others will want to snuggle in with a loved one and have sex. No two people are alike.

There are those of us who feel the need for closeness and reassurance when someone has died. Intimacy can give us that at times.   Sex transports us.   It reassures us of physical contact. Sex releases physical tension.   When you are grieving your body tenses up in ways you may not even realize at the time. Focusing on physical and sexual contact and pleasure releases that tension.   Orgasms release tension as well. We release chemicals from our brain including oxytocin and serotonin that result in feeling peaceful. Sex can have a calming effect in the midst of the storm.   It provides a sense of intimacy and closeness that we need.

SEVERE SENSE OF HOPELESSNESS

Hope is a powerful and necessary internal mechanism that help keep us moving forward in our lives. We can do almost anything for a short period of time because we have hope things will get better.   In the sudden death of loved ones this sense of hope can be stolen from us.   As with most symptoms of grief, this will take time to heal. Create a positive support system around you so you don't feel alone. Talk to someone about your feelings.   Allow them to provide feedback that supports you in your process. It is imperative to share your feelings with someone or more than one support person. You could talk with a close friend or family member, a pastor or rabbi, a hospice worker, a social worker therapist or other support person in your life. I would encourage you to talk to the Source of All aka as the God of your understanding. You may be surprised how creating a relationship with a Higher Power helps facilitate your healing.

   Tapping into hope is the same as tapping into the Love that is in the Universe. Love heals.   HOPE stands for **Hold On Pain Ends**. Keep hope alive in your life.

FORGIVENESS HEALS!

FEELING NUMB

It is a natural occurrence for us to feel numb until we can process our losses. Actually, we can experience feeling devastating loss and numbness simultaneously. Our bodies are amazing pieces of mystery that were created to keep us balanced and have a state of well-being. The numbness as a gift from our Creator to be able to handle the depth and breadth of your pain. It gives us some time to process the intensity of the emotional loss. Trust the process.

SELF MEDICATION

You have been reading throughout this book that self-medicating behavior is risky behavior. It is a route to feeling less pain for a temporary period of time. It may be over eating, over drinking, taking drugs, over spending or some other forms of over doing and being out of balance so you can feel better and distracted from your pain. This does not work in the long run. It masks the pain that you are going to have to feel. t adds additional layers of pain to have to work through.

MEMORY CHALLENGES

Grief pulls from all our resources at any time. Inattention to detail is often found to be a symptom of grief. Too much data is being processed through the brain and into your energetic fields and you find yourself on overload. Choose not to make any serious decisions until some time has passed. For example, do not choose to buy or sell property while grieving. Do not make decisions that involve giving away money in any form. Do not remarry because you feel lonely. Keep things simple. One day at a time in decision making. Make lists of things that need to get done. Make a decision not to try to do more than you are able to do on your list. Be gentle and kind to yourself. You are not losing your mind. You are not losing your ability to remember. You are grieving.

ISOLATION

Isolation is a major problem for grieving people.   It's not a natural tendency.   It's a learned behavior. Actively choosing to isolate yourself while you are grieving has its benefits and its challenges.   Grieving does have a component of needing to have some time alone to yourself to cope with the changes. On the other side of the coin are the concerns that self-isolation brings when you are alone too long. Finding the balance is a one moment at a time - one day at a time situation. Each unique individual has their own set of circumstances, cultural beliefs and religious beliefs.   The bottom line is that if you are isolating yourself too much you can lost deep into your grief. That is not healthy. The antidote to isolation is participation. It is important to share your thoughts and feelings with those you trust. Make it safe to talk openly about some of the sad or painful things you feel.   Part of the healing process is telling your story repeatedly. Go for a short walk every day. Start motivating yourself, albeit gently, to walk to the corner and back.   Add more steps as you are able. Note things that you like to experience like the winds gently blowing, colorful flowers on the path, a neighbor's dog, the clouds in the sky or any other thing that you enjoy. Feel the feeling of enjoying something you experience as good.

SLEEPING

Sleeping normally after a loss is unlikely. Your body needs more rest than usual. Wanting to sleep is a natural mechanism intended to slow you down and encourage you to care for your body. Sleeping is a great way to hide from the pain you are feeling. Many folks report that while sleeping they dream that their loved ones are still alive.   It is comforting to feel like things are normal and safe. Waking up to the reality of your personal grief is like waking up to your own personal nightmare. Sleep can be healing and restoring.   When you are grieving you usually feel under-rested, stressed and overwhelmed.   In reality, you have special needs.   The emotions of grief are often body felt experiences.   You find that you are grieving your life losses from the inside out.   You are probably finding that your normal sleep patterns have been thrown off.   You may find that you are having difficulty getting to sleep.   It is more likely that you may wake up early in the morning and have trouble getting back to sleep.   You may also find yourself getting tired more quickly.   You can wake up tired even at the start of the day.   Physical self-care takes time, discipline, mindfulness, and discernment.   Naps are suggested if possible in your schedule.

In the present moment, your "Divine Spark or Life Force Energies" that which gives your life meaning and purpose - may feel like it has turned completely off. Your spirit, your "Life Force energies or Divine Spark" can and will be re-ignited over time. You can find renewed meaning and even joy in your life.

INABILITY TO FUNCTION WELL DAILY

The stress of grief can suppress your immune system and your concentration. It can make you more vulnerable to physical problems. If you have an existing health challenge it may become worse. Self-medicating will only make things worse.

Attention to detail may not be available to you until later on in your grieving process. Right now you may not feel in control of how your body is responding. Your body is communicating with you about the special needs it has right now. Giving attention to your physical symptoms will allow you to discover your body's natural intelligence. Be gentle with yourself. Do not expect so much out of yourself. Give yourself a chance to work through the grief process.

Choose to not make any major decisions right after a huge loss. Major decisions could include selling your home, moving to a new location, and getting re-married. Sometimes we want to attempt to create a new way of living to feel better. We then make poor choices based out of irrational thinking.

At the risk of sounding repetitive give yourself time to grieve.

ANGER

Anger shows up once you are feeling safe enough to know you will probably survive whatever comes. At first, the fact you lived through the loss is probably surprising to you.

Anger is secondary to wounded-ness. In others words you cannot get angry until you have first felt hurt. In grief, you are hurting from the inside out. It is a feeling of vulnerability and feeling raw. It is a gut wrenching ache so deep inside of yourself that there are moments that you wonder if you will ever feel normal again. That kind of pain is not an easy fix. Heartache is painful. Anger usually happens when we feel helpless and powerless. A sense of being in a dreamlike state is very unsettling. We have been taught in our culture to try not to feel pain. I am telling you to feel your pain.

When your pain becomes too unbearable for your psyche to handle it will shift to anger. It is a naturally built in response in our mind.

Anger feels better! Anger burns energy. Anger holds a higher energy level than grief and sorrow. Anger allows us to cope with our pain in a different energetic form. Anger allows us the illusion that we are in control of our lives and our body. Anger gives us permission to be a martyr, a victim or the ability to drown in our own self-pity. You may be shocked when the intensity of your anger is in direct proportion to the intensity of your love for the one who has died. This is an incredible insight when you understand it.

When we are grieving, anger is another indicator of how much we loved the person who died. If you feel anger over your loved one's death, you owe no one an apology for your grief or your anger. It is part of your personal grief process.

Anger can stem from a feeling of abandonment because of a death or loss. Sometimes we're angry at a Higher Power, at the God of your understanding, for taking your loved one at such an inconvenient time, at the doctors who cared for your loved one and toward life in general. We don't understand why we are angry! As if knowing why our loved one was taken would make us feel any better! We live in Divine Time. We do not always get to understand in the present moment what has transpired or why.

Anger is a normal part of grief. It is a foot bridge of strength and energy that leads us to self-healing. Anger tells you that you are alive.

You loved someone very much. You are angry because now that person is dead. Anger is progress because it means you are feeling the emotions of grief needed in order to heal. The more we honor our loss by allowing ourselves to feel anger, the more healing we will do.   Explore your anger. Make your anger work for you.   The more you allow your feelings to surface the more of yourself you will find.

Anger can cause us to do or say things now that we will regret later, resulting in even more pain. Be wise with your anger. Do not allow yourself to go off on others because you are feeling angry. Angry energy will not go away on its own. It must be released.

Unacknowledged anger grows larger and larger until it erupts. Ignoring your anger never works. Adding alcohol or drugs to the mix can only exacerbate the situation.

Alcohol is a depressant by nature.   The more you can understand your anger and how you react when you're mad the more you can make changes that allow for your healing.

People will criticize your anger because it is uncomfortable to be around. The problems arise when you misdirect anger unfairly at those around you or turn it towards ourselves. Anger turned inward can create physical and emotional problems such as heart attacks, ulcers, high blood pressure, anxiety, depression and self-medication.

Anger can also be a constructive force for good. Anger can be focused to help facilitate positive changes for others. Think about how changes have come in our legal system by folks who were hurting and then got angry.

They focused their energy to create organizations and laws to help others.

Families of the 911 Attack created foundations to support others who were hurting or harmed. Mothers Against Drunk

Driving used their anger to create a powerful lobby for new protection laws.

NOTES

CHAPTER THREE

COMPLICATED GRIEF

Complicated Grief is also known as Traumatic Grief or Pathological Grief. It is defined as grief that is getting in the way of coping with the death of someone you love. Complicated grief can also be defined as the challenge involved in the healing process that normally occurs, after even a sudden and terrible loss, goes somehow awry. It develops a complication, like an infection in a wound. Individuals with Complicated Grief may find that they are unable to accept the death and that their feelings remain very strong and persistent. In addition, there may be certain types of disturbing ideas that seem to inhibit the natural process of gradual diminishing grief intensity. Grief isn't working and the bereaved person is "stuck" in the grieving process. When this happens, grief intensity remains high and adjustment does not occur.

It is causing you to have trouble functioning in your life on a daily basis. It may also be defined as more than one loss in a short time period of your life. The pain is unrelenting and you feel as if it is hopeless to go on. Acute grief is a disconcerting experience.

It is normal to get stuck in an emotional place that doesn't move us forward in acute and complicated grief. It could be a sudden or traumatic loss that is the main reason that one person gets stuck. It could be a prior history of mood disorders, or anxiety, or a trauma, and or an early life loss. It could be because somebody is not able to deal with their emotions. Someone who is very avoidant of allowing themselves to feel those emotions can get stuck. Certain types of loss, such as the death of a child or a sudden, unexpected or violent death can increase the chances of developing complicated grief.

Complicated grief is characterized by symptoms including marked depression, anxiety, panic attacks, preoccupation with the deceased, disbelief, longing, anger, guilt, withdrawal, and avoidance that continue for 6 month or more after a loss. These symptoms can cause substantial distress and have been associated with impaired quality of life, poor medical outcomes, and increased rates of suicide. There is a persistent, intense yearning for the person who has died. Another symptom is withdrawal from friends and family. There are intrusive thoughts and a preoccupation with memories of the deceased loved one. Strong emotions that are hard to control and troubling thoughts related to the death are some the symptoms along with avoidance of the situations that hold painful memories.

Many families who lost a loved one or more than one loved one in the September 11th attacks on the United States had complicated grief.   One clear blue sky autumn morning they sent their loved ones off to work. Thousands did not come home. The emotional shock to their support systems and the families was horrendous. Some people refused to go get their partner's cars at the train station as they fully expected them to come home driving the car into the driveway. They spent hours and days calling hospitals and emergency rooms searching frantically for some tiny morsel of hope to believe that their loved one was alive.

They walked all over the Port Authority areas and New York docks looking for some information that would indicate that their loved one was still alive.   Some folks refused to believe that their loved one was murdered. The pregnant women who became widows who were due to deliver were especially wounded. Their pain was palpable. Fear gripped them. Reality was no longer reality.

Life had changed in a few seconds. Nothing was ever going to be the same. Yet they were still pregnant. Some wanted to die. Some were so heartbroken that their unborn children were grieving in the womb. Severe cases of Post-Partum Depression with Post Traumatic Stress Disorder were diagnosed. There existed this great disbelief (also known as denial) that this trauma could happen at all and specifically to them. Suicidal ideation was at an all-time high within that culture and community. The pain appeared endless. Hope was hard for some folks to have. A significantly high number of the family survivors were put on anti-anxiety and anti-depressant medicines. Many folks were diagnosed with Post Traumatic Stress Disorder.

Major Depression Disorder and Chronic Complicated Grief. Remember though that HOPE means **H**old **O**n **P**ain **E**nds.

NOTES

CHAPTER FOUR

TERMINAL ILLNESS AND GRIEF

It can be said that we are all terminal at some point. Terminal Illness gives us an idea of the time table of life for a person we love. Our grieving begins as soon as we hear the words "terminal illness". The grief process is quite different for a person who has a loved one who has been labeled terminal than that of a young couple who lose their baby to Sudden Infant Death Syndrome. They both are going to wreak havoc with your heart and spirit.

However, one provides a person with time to prepare somewhat for an ending of a life (anticipating grief) and the other is a sudden traumatic event.

Anticipatory grief means grappling with and grieving a loss before it completely unfolds. We feel anticipatory grief when we know someone we care about is seriously ill and is unlikely to live very long.

Devastating losses include lack of ability to drive, lack of independence, lack of ability to care take oneself and impaired physical, mental and emotional abilities.

There are many losses to grieve long before the person is diagnosed as terminally ill; for the person who is dying as well as for family and friends. When someone has a serious illness it is a scary situation for all involved. Just as with grief after a death, family and friends may feel a multitude of different emotions as they adjust to the new situation if facing a terminal illness of their lives. Typical emotions beyond grief at this time include:

- Sorrow

- Anxiety

- Anger

- Acceptance

- Depression

- Denial

- Attempting bargaining with the God of your understanding

- Fear that the words you need to say will not come out right

You may feel closer and determined to make the time you have left count more once you become aware of the situation. Perhaps you are terribly anxious about what's to come. You may be so focused on last-resort treatments that you continue to compartmentalize your thoughts until the end. Although not everyone experiences anticipatory grief, all of these feelings are

normal for those who do. You may find the
following steps comforting:

- Talk with sympathetic friends or family
  members who have weathered similar
  situations.

- Join a hospice support group online or in
  person

- Talk/counsel with a Spiritual Leader
  such as a Pastor, Rabbi, Imam

- Talk/counsel with the Hospital Chaplain

- Talk with the Hospice Staff

- Read books or listen to tapes designed
  for caregivers.

A terminal illness offers you time to say "I
love you," to share your appreciation, and to
make amends when necessary. When
death occurs unexpectedly, people often
regret not having had a chance to do these

things.   It is as important for you as it is to them in most cases. Never lose an opportunity to make peace and provide loving compassionate communication with your loved one.   Once they are gone you have lost your opportunity.

Sometimes it's easier for a dying person to share what he or she fears and explore it with someone other than a family member. That is where hospice workers, hospital chaplains, nurturing nurses, community spiritual leaders and social workers can help so much!   While you are working on your grief they need to be working on their grief.

Sometimes, dying people hold on to life because they sense that others aren't ready to let them go. Tell your loved one it's all right to let go when he or she is ready to do so.   Tell them to "go toward the light".   The assurance that you will be able to carry on; perhaps to help children grow or to fulfill other shared dreams may offer enormous relief. Sometimes they wait until you have left the room to transition to the Other Side. Perhaps they felt you couldn't be there when they were ready to go. It is an intuitive thing for them.

My mother laid in the hospital room dying for two and one half weeks. It was an intense emotional time for us all. I talked with her, prayed with her and sang to her. I stayed with her around the clock attending to her every need. We both knew the end was near. Folks came to visit her from the small rural community that she had lived in for almost 86 years. She had been a teacher for fifty years. Generations of family members in our community had been taught by her.

As word moved through our little town and county the visitors lined up in the hallway to pay their respects to her while she was still alive. Each had hugs, tears and prayers with her. My Mama was a prayer warrior. She had prayer with every single person who came to pay their respects to her! Many folks had a request for her. "Please tell my daddy that I am sorry I was not there when he passed over." "Please tell my Mother I found the Lord." It truly was amazing to observe this spiritual connection between my Mama and her friends.

Sometimes I became a bit protective of her quickly depleting energy when there were too many visitors in a row. I did not want her to wear down too quickly. There was an internal conflict for me in how much to let her be bombarded by loved ones who had thoughts and wishes for her and how much time would I have left of her for me. Spiritual journeys teach us how to share and how to love.

She knew she was going to transition to the Other Side. She told me five days before she went into the hospital that I needed to prepare because she was going. She told me to "be strong. Always eat an aspirin before you go to bed. Stay in my faith and trust God." Always, always, always, she told me how much she loved me. I am blessed to have had that time with her.

The morning before her body stopped the sunshine came streaming through the hospital windows. It had been raining for most of that week so the sunshine was truly welcomed. My Mama opened up her eyes and looked at me in disbelief. She said" Jannie, how did all those angels get on the wall?" I told her they were there to take her home. She smiled the most peaceful smile, told me she loved me and closed her eyes for the last time. Her body fought on for about 14 more hours. I knew she had left with the angels the afternoon before.

Did I have heartache? Oh yes, my heart ached! I sobbed and sobbed. I was nauseous and thought I would vomit for a few days especially through the funeral service and wake. Simultaneously, I had been able to process much of my grief as her terminal illness came closer and closer to taking her away. I was able to see that she was at peace.

She was no longer fighting the illness that stole her last breath. No longer was she in pain. I loved her enough to allow my surrender to her process. I loved her enough to accept that she needed to leave and be at peace. Was it easy? Absolutely not. I felt like a motherless child. I felt abandoned on some cosmic level. However, she came to me in so many different forms in the days ahead. I felt so grateful to be able to hold a sacred place for her in her final days. There was a tumultuous mix of emotions that continued for at least a year. Tears were an everyday occurrence. I was at peace with her passing. My sorrow was for myself. For so long after she had passed, every time I had something great that I would have been sharing with her I would pick up the phone to call her and reality would hit again. She is gone. Next there were tears - then acceptance.

This is not always the way things pan out. Folks don't always get to make peace and say their goodbyes. Know this: Hearing is the last sense to go. Even if you think they cannot hear you they can. Their soul can feel you too. Never give up hope of communication. If you were close with them on this Earth plane then you don't even have to be in the room or at the hospital at all. We live in time and space. When we transition we move out of time and space and into unlimited realms beyond our imaginations. They heard your thoughts and prayers wherever you were while they were transitioning. Be sure about this truth!

A few words about family during grief work. If there ever is a time for dysfunction to show up in a family structure count on it happening at a death. I wish I could say all families get along and love each other especially at a time like this. However, it is much more highly likely that all hell can and will break loose when death roars its ugly head. That is because greed and fear are chasing right behind. Be prepared for anything and everything!

A vital part of the grieving process is the rituals to bring closure for the family and friends of the deceased. In America, we usually have some time of Memorial or Celebrations of Life Services that includes a wake or viewing of the body and then a Funeral Service with a Graveside Service to follow for those who are of the Christian faith. There are also Crematory Services. You may sit Shiva. You may hold a wake in your home or in a funeral home.

Now, as we have discussed previously, everyone copes differently. Some don't

cope at all. Add alcohol to the dynamic.
Add greed. Add drugs - prescription or
illegal. Add fear. Add step family dynamics.
Add sibling rivalry. Add divorce to the mix.
Add guilt. If there is a will add more greed.
Add manipulation of fragile family members.
Add shame. Add the stinking thinking of the
"she loved you more than me" ideology to
the mix. It gets very ugly. You are grieving
and now you have to add some or all of this
to your experience. It is incredibly painful!

It is important here to remind you that
volume does not increase comprehension.
So if all else fails, do not start screaming at
each other. No one wins. Just walk away.
Do not take what other say and do
+++personally. It is not about you at all. It
is all about them. Protect yourself by
staying out of the fracas. Remember there
are others who are deeply wounded and
show it by acting out behavior.

CHAPTER FIVE

THE WOUNDED SELF

It is hard to admit we are wounded. It is hard to admit we have lost our way. The truth is that some of us have never truly found our way yet. Some people are still searching. The good news is that if you are still searching you have not given up hope in finding your way down your path. There is always hope even when it is your experience not to have been seeking it. That is called grace.

I can speak from my personal experience and from those of others I have worked with over my thirty eight years of working with people. The Wounded Self has these symptoms:

- Lack of confidence

- Unchecked rage

- Uncomfortable in new environments

- Feeling as if they are not enough

- Fatigue

- Depression

- Digestive issues

- High levels of irritability

- Moodiness

- Queasy stomach conditions

- Profound sadness without understanding why

- Feelings of nervousness and anxiety

- Irrational fear

- A tendency to have headaches and or joint pain

- Lack of flexibility in decision making

- Lack of accountability in regard to your actions

- Willingness to blame others

- A sense of unreasonable entitlement

- Low self esteem

- Deeply imbedded self-loathing

- Relationships that are conditional versus unconditionally loving relationships
- Fears of abandonment

- A strong sense of betrayal by others

- A desire to be in control whenever possible

- heightened feelings of guilt and shame

- heightened feelings of resentment and embarrassment

- A false self-put on for the public to see

- Codependency issues

- Addictive personalities

- Complicated grief

- And fear based thinking

You do not have to have all these symptoms to qualify. While you are reading this list you know which ones you resonate with and feel.

You will know if you self-qualify by your own truth. I am sure that you are either a person that is dealing with these issues or love a person who is dealing with these issues or you would not be reading this book.

You are in pain when you are emotionally wounded. You ache emotionally, as in heartache. You ache physically as in body aches and joint pain. You may suffer from Irritable Bowel Disorder or Crohn's Disease. You are afraid. You lie. You lie about your lying. You act as if you are a bully.

You demand to be in control of situations. You have very little self-confidence because you do not believe in yourself. You feel as if you are a failure in life at times. You do not feel strong an empowered. You feel fragile and afraid more often than not. You question your own decisions. You incur high levels of self-doubt. Does this resonate with you? You overcompensate for this by acting as if you are in control. It is a facade. You are absolutely not in control of yourself and your feelings. There is not a strong true point of personal power within you. You have no idea of what personal empowerment is when you are struggling. It is completely out of your experience.

Tiredness is your regular state of mind. It takes a tremendous amount of energy to get through each day because you have not yet found how to transform your fears and anxieties into power. It is likely that you do not eat as nutritiously as you could. It is likely that you have a high intake of white sugars and junk food. You do not feed your body well enough to fuel yourself in a healthy manner. Perhaps you take prescription drugs for emotional issues. Perhaps you drink too much alcohol or take illegal drugs to self-medicate. Bottom line is that you do not take care of yourself. Why? Self-love and self-care are low on your priorities list!

Most of you transfer your sense of safety to external controls. Your locus of control is questionable. Often you make up a story about what personal success looks like for you then you fail to make the grade. Purchasing lots of things to make yourself feel better about yourself is a top priority. If you have the nicest house, car, vacation, clothes, jewelry etc. makes you feel better about yourself. Commonly you find yourself choosing the role of victim or martyr. You find this easier than choosing to be accountable for your actions or lack of actions.

You appear lethargic or lazy to some. In truth, you are paralyzed with fear that you throw an attitude with others rather than deal with yourself. Sarcasm prevails rather than compliments, compassion and kindness.

You lack desire to learn internal controls because that would take motivation and desire. You are most likely not going to make changes until you are pushed to your limit and are frightened beyond your comfort zone.

Change happens when we are ready to surrender to the process. **Change happens when the pain to stay in the same situation is bigger than the perceived pain you think it is going to be for change.** Change happens when your desperation becomes greater than your comfort zone or your discomfort zone.

What does this have to do with grief you ask? Everything. When grief hits it doesn't care if you feel solid as a rock or as fragile as a leaf blowing in the autumn wind. You need to know who you are to better handle your grief.   You will know who you are once grief has taken hold of you, fine-tuned your rough edges and spit you back out into the world.

Look at it this way, if you are not able to handle your emotions on a happy day what are you going to do when you are faced with a traumatic and unforeseen tragedy?

Life can change in the blink of an eye. What belief system are you using to create your life? Is it a positive Spirit based thinking system built with heavy doses of faith, belief in a Source greater than yourself?   Do you have a sense of wonder in how the Universe actually works?   Do you know that there is a Divine Spark inside of you that is call the Life-Force Energy? This is where love abides within you!

If your idea of coping with stress is to drink until you are sloppy and dangerous to be on the road then grief is going to roll all over you.   Grief matters.   How you handle your life will tell you much about how you will handle your grief.

Grief has such amazing power to transform a person from the inside out.   You must go with the flow of life and of grief. Grief is a significant part of life.   Wounded people have a much harder time coping with the torrential emotions and waves of grief. It is as if the perfect storm hits and you are not prepared.

I encourage you to slowly and calmly look at how you handle your decision making about yourself and yourself in relationship to life.   It is a choice to see yourself as wounded.   It is a choice to see yourself as empowered.   The significant difference between the two polar opposites is the spiritual transformation that occurs within you over time. Are you open to growing and changing?   Does that make you afraid to consider?   Can you face those fears and move forward anyway? I am not speaking of a religious experience.   I am speaking of a spiritual experience. A transformation within brought about by learning to love yourself. One way or the other grief is going to change you. In that transformation, grief has less power to harm and more power to heal. Grief can become your friend!

NOTES

CHAPTER SIX

SUICIDE

Suicide cuts across all sex, age, gender, religions, sexual orientations and economic barriers. People of all ages complete suicide. Men and women, as well as young children, complete suicide. Gays, lesbians, heterosexuals, transgendered folk, the rich as well as the poor kill themselves. Catholics, Jews, Christians, Metaphysicians, Hindi, Muslims and Agnostics kill themselves. No one is immune to this tragedy. No one! Asking "WHY?" will haunt you. Let that go.

We know that everyone has a reason. Sometimes we get to know the reason. Sometimes we are left to create why on our own. Our imaginations can make up incredible stories when left to our own minds.

The first point I want to make about suicide is that it was NOT your fault that your loved one decided to leave us. There was nothing you could have done. They made their mind up on their own. Reread these sentences again and again until you get this truth in your thinking clearly.

No matter how long and hard you search for a reason, you won't be able to answer the "WHY" that haunts you. Each suicide is individual, regardless of the "whys". Sometimes there are no apparent causes. There may be no way you will completely understand the suicide victim's thought process. That is a lot to cope with and stay sane. You MUST let go and let God handle this part of the experience for you and for the loved one.

It might have been a quick snap reaction to a situation. In reaction, we are not responding. We are reacting. We are not thinking. We are emoting. Add alcoholism or drug addiction to the mix. It becomes more likely. Add mental illness to the situation. The percentages go up on suicide. Factors have a place in the understanding of the situations. Take an active alcoholic who is drinking and is also depressed and the percentages go up on suicide. Had the person been sober they may not have acted in the same manner. Overdoses are usually not on purpose. The addict took too much and in their effort to self-medicate went too far. It happens every day.

Shock is the first reaction to death. You may feel numb for a while. You may feel totally overwhelmed with emotions that are so intense you think you cannot breathe. You may be unable to follow a normal daily routine. This shock can be healthy. It can protect you from the initial pain of the loss. It may help you get through funeral arrangements and services. It may last a few days or go on for several weeks. Take some time to be alone if that is what you want. Isolation is not good for too long. Your family may need you to be present with them longer than usual. Your physical presence may be needed for them to feel more comfortable in an oh so not comfortable situation.

Grieving together is healing. It is also important to be with other people. It may be helpful for you to return to your normal routine as soon as you are able.

It is very likely that you may feel angry, guilty, and grief stricken after the initial shock of being told that someone you love has killed himself/herself. These feelings may overwhelm you all at once. They may show up immediately. They may surface in the weeks, months, and years ahead. You may handle them well initially only to have them return for no apparent reason. Grief comes in waves. These feelings, and the helplessness that comes with them, will pass. Try to understand and accept the things you feel. What you are feeling is healthy. It is all part of the healing and coping process. It is normal to be incredibly grief stricken with this loss. Be gentle with yourself. We are all here together, to love and help one another. Let yourself be loved by others.

You are going to experience a whirlwind of emotions as a relative or loved one coping with a suicide death. You are likely to experience anger often directed at the deceased. You may ask "How could he do this to me?" "What was he thinking?"

Blame becomes an option for a period of time while you are processing this life experience. If the deceased was receiving psychiatric or medical care you may ask, "Why didn't they prevent it? The doctors did not see this coming!"

You may find yourself angry with the God of your understanding for "allowing this to happen." Many people blame God. Then they use that as an excuse to not participate in religious life or a spiritual life. Others cling to God for hope and help to move through this incredible pain that does not feel like it will ever let up. If you are angry with God, share your feelings with someone who cares and will listen.

The God of my understanding is the only One prepared to handle all your anger, resentment, sorrow and pain. I submit that there is a God of Love that is there to support you in your time of need.

The anger may be self-directed – "What could I have done?" or "Why wasn't I there?" This happens so often for parents and spouses. The truth is you did not nor will you ever have enough power to change someone's mind if they have made this decision. Reaction nor response, you cannot blame yourself for someone else's actions. There is nothing you could have done or said to stop what happened. It was their choice and life path. Reread the previous paragraph numerous times.

Don't try to deny or hide your anger, grief, rejection or resentment. They are natural consequences of the seemingly endless pain you feel. It will eventually come out in other possibly more destructive ways and it will prolong your healing process. You need to find someone you can talk to about these feelings. Usually your pastor, minister, rabbi, social worker or close friend can listen and be a healing part of your process.

No one will have any magic answers for you. No one will be able to make you hurt less. Your healing and coping process requires that you talk about your feelings, about all the sadness, anger, hurt, rejection and guilt you are carrying around inside you. You can heal yourself however.

Healing does come easier if you have a God of your understanding to vent to.

You may need to release your anger physically; take long brisk walks or any exercise that is reasonable for your physical capabilities. Using a tennis racket on your bed mattress does wonders for pent up frustration.

You might want to start a journal and write regularly in it. It may prove to be a valuable tool in your healing process.

Don't deny your feelings. Talk about it, think about it, and constructively deal with it.

Friends may provide all the emotional support you need or you may want to join a mutual support group and meet with others who have experienced the suicide of a loved one. The suicide hotline in your area may be able to offer you some understanding and support over the telephone. Often these hotlines are answered 24 hours a day by people especially trained to help you through the rough spots. They will understand your feelings and help you find ways to work things out.

It is normal to be devastated.   It is normal to want to understand "why"? It is normal to want to know all the facts prior to the suicide. All that effort will still not lessen your pain. There are many people who hold the thought that suicide is selfish and cowardly. They believe that the person with the suicidal ideation is in pain but does not want to deal with it to the extent of doing the emotional and spiritual work to attain peace.

Ultimately, you have to go to a place of gratitude for the time you had with that person. You have to be thankful for the memories. You have to put your energy and your attention on the living. You can pray for the soul of the deceased if that makes you feel better. You have to make choices to go on and live for the now moment.   Let the past stay in the past.   Remember the good times.

Let go and Let God.

Mental illness, drug and alcohol addiction are real illnesses. I have spoken to numerous theologians and spiritual leaders who have assured me that they believe that those who have committed suicide under the influence of these conditions did not do so of their free will. They will get the help that they need from their Creator. They are not condemned to hell.

Just as this book was going to print I got a telephone call telling me a close personal friend and former partner had shot herself in the head. It was shocking to hear and more shocking to feel. She was a highly trained psychotherapist with an abundant life. She lived alone in a custom built, to her specifications, multimillion dollar home with extended land so she could control who lived near her, no financial challenges due to a huge inheritance from her parents, new car paid in full, swimming pool and hot tub just outside her glass doors and an active practice. She appeared to be living the good life we often aspire to. However, depression eats away at the mind and spirit of anyone it can attach itself to.

Underneath the facade was a devastated little girl who had been abused her entire young life by her mother. Her father looked the other way in a passive mode in an effort not to have his wife's angst aimed at him. Wounds that did not heal over sixty years came out yesterday with a single gut shot wound to the head.

No one will ever know what was playing out in her mind. Clearly depression had won the battle. She called a friend to come pick up her little dog and said she would be in the back yard. The friend showed up, got the dog and found her still warm but breathless body in the back yard.

Suicide...it can happen to anyone given a specific set of circumstances. Some event or a series of events have to happen for our loved ones to choose this choice. It becomes a rational option for those who are considering it. The hardest thing to do is not ask yourself "why?". As discussed previously that is a dangerous and slippery downward slide for those who are left on this Earth to deal with the loss.

I played detective for a few hours attempting to learn all the facts I could get from folks about who had talked to her recently, what was her mood like, did she have any traumatic events in this current time period to trigger her to do this most selfish act. I got answers to my questions. The reality of the situation was she was depressed, in physical pain, emotional pain and spiritual pain. Depression allows your mind to see things in a darker light. The answer seems simple to those who are in this mind set. They want the pain they are feeling to end. They cannot or do not see a way to make that happen. So they create a way out of their pain. They do not reach out for support or help. They are looking for a way to be in control of this last act in their life.

I wonder if they think of the others who will find them. Do they think of their families and how they will react to this significant loss? Do they take into account the long term effects of their loved ones lives? I don't think that comes into play by the time they are planning this out.

I think that our loved ones, some with incredibly warm hearts and spirits, get to a place where their thinking is that the only way out is to literally and physically check out. This is how suicide rears its ugly head.

Here are some of the situations I have found myself in since I was given this news:

- I have wanted to scream a deep, piercing scream but nothing would come out.

- I have wanted to cry but I feel too numb to cry yet.

- Nausea has set in with a vengeance.

- I have flashes in my mind of good and bad memories from our time together.

- I see her in my minds' eye.

- I wonder what her last thoughts were.

- I wonder if she left a note.

- I want to tell myself I could have helped her; but, it is not true.

It has taken a long time to learn that I cannot fix the world. Not for my children nor for my friends. It is their path--their journey.

To some this will sound cold and non-emotional. This is not the case. How does it serve you to hold on to the thoughts that you are/were responsible for the suicide of another person? How sane is that? How do we know what they agreed to on the Other Side with Source Energy? Perhaps they came into this lifetime to help others learn forgiveness or compassion. It is hard to say for sure.

I was raised to serve. My parents taught us well that we take care of each other. Watch over each other. There were no lessons on how to cope if my brother commits suicide.

This can really mess with your mind. Be gentle with yourself. The questions will keep coming until they don't. The answers are far harder to find. Acceptance can give us peace in a chaotic situation.

Once they shift their mindset to checking out, no matter how long or short a thought pattern it is, they are going to check out.

Our job is to accept that this is the truth. We are powerless to their choices.

Our job is to love each other. It is not to control or judge another. This is a very hard fact to get clear in our minds. We want to attach some of our wishes and beliefs to others even though it is not our place. It

doesn't matter if they were our lover, our
son, our daughter or a friend.

Our response is to forgive them for their
actions. This is not an easy task. Some of us
want to grab the mantle of victim to cope with
situation. Bringing attention to ourselves is
another opportunity to get attention for our
pain. Coping mechanisms are different for
everyone. Our ability to handle grief varies
from person to person. Our experience in
handling life and grief varies person to
person. Our spiritual consciousness varies
from person to person.

Forgive them we must. Our life depends
upon it. We cannot move forward in a good
orderly direction (god) without accepting
what is and surrendering to the process. I
think that we have some influence on how
we choose to respond to situations in life.
We don't, however, get to control the life we
get. We can work at manifesting a particular
type of life situation.

Living life on life's terms is the prerequisite for success and serenity.

NOTES

CHAPTER SEVEN

CHILDREN AND GRIEF

Children have magical thinking. The concept of death is not real to them until they are much older. Talking to children about death must be geared to their developmental level, respectful of their cultural norms and sensitive to their capacity to understand the situation. Until kids are about 5 or 6 years old, their view of the world is very literal. So explain death in basic and concrete terms. If the loved one was ill or elderly, you might explain that the person's body wasn't working anymore and the doctors couldn't fix it. If someone dies suddenly, like in an accident, you might explain what happened; that because of this very sad event, the person's body stopped working. You may have to explain that "dying" or "dead" means that the body stopped working. They do not understand dead or dying in terms we understand as adults.

Children this young often have a hard time understanding that all people and living things eventually die. They have a hard time understanding that it's final and they won't come back. Cartoon hero's always live. So even after you've explained this, children may continue to ask where their loved one is or when the person is returning. Continue to calmly reiterate that the person has died and can't come back.

Avoid telling children that the loved one "went away" or "went to sleep" or even that your family "lost" the person. Because young kids think so literally, such phrases might make them afraid to go to sleep or fearful whenever someone goes away. This is similar to when children are taught the "Now I lay me down to sleep" prayer that goes on to say "if I should dies before I wake" and cause children to fear going to sleep.

Children from the ages of about 6 to 10 start to grasp the finality of death. They deal best with death when given accurate, simple, clear, and honest explanations about what happened. Keep it simple.

Children are people too. Their responses are basic skills that they have been taught by their families and their culture. Expect the following responses which may waiver back and forth as they find their way to cope:

- **Emotional shock** - at times an apparent lack of feelings, which serve to help the child detach from the pain of the moment

- **Regressive (immature) behaviors,** such as needing to be rocked or held, difficulty separating from parents or significant others, and/or needing to sleep in parent's bed or an apparent difficulty completing tasks well within the child's ability level

- **Explosive emotions** and acting out behavior temper tantrums/screaming/ rage/ fear based responses) that reflect the child's internal feelings of anger, terror, frustration and helplessness.

Acting out may reflect insecurity and a way to seek control over a   situation for which they have little or no control.

- **Asking the Same Questions Repeatedly** - Understanding the finality of death takes time and practice.

- **Challenges with Digestive Issues -** Stomach aches are common. Soiling their pants is not uncommon. It is the only thing they can control when they feel that everything is out of control.

- **Nightmares or Night Terrors** - If the child is very close to the deceased you will need to   be prepared for nightmares or night terrors where they are losing the loved one from a bad guy or scary monster. Reassure your child they are safe and that they are loved.

Stay with them until they get back to sleep. Give extra nurturing as needed. Remember they are little ones and it is scary!

Here are some suggestions for helping children cope and move forward.

- Keep a light on in the bedroom when they sleep for as long as it is needed. When they can handle turn the light off in the bedroom and move the light to the hall.

- Do not be surprised if your child says that the loved one came to see them in their bedroom. It does happen! More on that later in this book!

- Try to get the children back on their regular schedule so that the comfort of ritual becomes comforting again. Feeling safe is paramount to getting back into their schedule.

- Make sure a nurturing adult is always with the children and that they are not left alone. Grief comes in waves.

- Just when you think they (and you for that matter) have a handle on grief a wave of emotion will arrive unexpected and they may be wiped out emotionally for a while.

- Don't allow the children to isolate. A little time alone is good. Too much time alone causes more challenges

- Allow them to feel listened to. Do not discount their experiences. They have a path to follow too!

- Teach them by example how to behave and respond in funeral homes, wakes and graveside services.

- It is important to recognize that all children are unique in their understanding of death and dying. This understanding depends on their developmental level, cognitive skills, personality characteristics, religious or spiritual beliefs, teachings by parents and significant others, input from the media, and previous experiences with death.

- Infants and Toddlers: The youngest children may perceive

that adults are sad, but have no real understanding of the meaning or significance of death.

- Preschoolers: Young children may deny death as a formal event and may see death as reversible. They may interpret death as a separation not a permanent condition. Preschool and even early elementary children may link certain events and magical thinking with the causes of death. For instance, as a result of the World Trade Center disaster, some children may imagine that going into tall buildings may cause someone's death.

- Early Elementary School: Children at this age (5-9) start to comprehend the finality of death. They begin to understand that certain circumstances may result in death. They can see that, if large planes crash into buildings, people in the planes and buildings will be killed. At this age, death is perceived as

- Something that happens to others, not to oneself or one's family.

- Middle School: Children at this level have the cognitive understanding to comprehend death as a final event that results in the cessation of all bodily functions. They may not fully grasp the abstract concepts discussed by adults or on the TV

- news but are likely to be guided in their thinking by a concrete understanding of justice.

- High School: Most teens will fully grasp the meaning of death in circumstances such as an automobile accident, illness and even the World Trade Center or Pentagon disasters. They may seek out friends and family for comfort or they may withdraw to deal with their grief. Teens (as well as some younger children) with a history of depression, suicidal behavior and chemical dependency are at particular risk for prolonged and serious grief reactions and may need more careful attention from home and school during these difficult times. Teach them to respect the situation and act appropriately.

Don't project your fears onto your children. They take their cues from the adults around them.

Try to limit their access to the recurring news and exposure to the tragedy over and over.

Understand that you can't completely shield them from what happened.

Model truth-telling and build trust with your children by letting them hear things, even hard things, from you directly.

NOTES

CHAPTER EIGHT

PARENTS AND THE LOSS OF A CHILD

The loss of a child is the most devastating experience a parent can face. Missing the child never goes away. A piece of yourself is lost and your future is forever changed. There is no pain as great as that of a parent whose child has died. It is not supposed to happen this way. The grief is so intense and the shock so deep that you feel like you are living in a dream state. You want the nightmare to end. Parents are simply not supposed to outlive their children. No parent is prepared for a child's death even if the child was terminally ill. Death changes every aspect of family life. It leaves enormous emptiness.

The grief journey has many emotional peaks and valleys and lasts far longer than society in   general recognizes. Each person's grief journey is unique. It is highly likely that you may find that you, your spouse and your family are all processing their grief at different speeds and in different ways.

There is no right or wrong way to grieve. You and your spouse will need to communicate clearly how you are feeling as you work through your grief individually, as a couple and as a family. Many marriages end because the couple quit talking. The pain is unbearable. You will feel raw and fragile. Make sure to accept that you are going to grieve differently.

The loss of a child isn't something you will get over; it is something you will learn to go through. When your child dies, the grief journey does not end in a week, a month or even a year. Don't let others' expectations be a guideline for your own progress. Be patient with yourself and with your family members. It also helps to be tolerant and accepting of the different approaches others may take.

In addition to grieving the death of your child, you may find that you grieve the loss of the hopes and dreams you had for your child. You may grieve the potential that will never be realized and the experiences you will never share like holidays, birthdays, Little League Sports, the Prom, High School graduation, watching them fall in love, go to college, weddings, and your future grandchildren. The pain of these losses will always be a part of you. Although grief is always profound when a child dies, some parents have an especially difficult time. For these parents the grief remains intense even as time passes. They feel it is impossible to return to normal life. This can become Complicated Grief.

Many grieving parents question whether life will hold any meaning for them. They wonder how they will survive the pain of their loss. Parents describe the feeling as having a hole in their heart that will never heal. They may blame themselves and say, "If only I had..." Grief can also vary greatly depending upon how the child died. While some losses are less visible, such as miscarriage, other experiences of loss are more traumatic, such as a suicide, a car accident, an illness, a murder or death during war.

Parents are intimately involved in the daily lives of young children. The death of an older child or adolescent is difficult because children at this age are beginning to reach their potential and become independent individuals. When an adult child dies, you not only lose a child, but, often a close friend. There is more loss as you lose a link to future grandchildren. You lose an irreplaceable source of emotional and practical support.

You may also feel that you have lost your identity as a parent if your only child dies. Parents may especially benefit from a support group where they can share their experiences with other parents who understand their grief and can offer hope.

Grief reactions following the death of a child are similar to those after other losses, but are often more intense and last longer. You may experience intense shock, confusion, disbelief, and denial, all of which can act as a cushion against the full impact. You may feel overwhelming sadness and despair to such a deep level such that facing daily tasks or even getting out of bed can seem impossible. You may feel extreme guilt as you may feel that you have failed as your child's protector. You may dwell on what you could have done differently to have saved him/her from the death. You may feel intense anger and feelings of bitterness and unfairness at a life left unfulfilled. Feelings of resentment toward parents with healthy children may show up for a period of time. Feelings that life has no meaning and that life is not fair may show up. You may find yourself wishing to be released from your pain and want to die to join your child. A desire to join your child who died is a normal and natural reaction to the pain you are experiencing. If these feelings become overwhelming and you begin to consider taking action, it is imperative that you seek professional support immediately.

You may dread being alone. It is normal to be questioning your faith and spiritual beliefs which then increases your pain. Many in grief find their faith to be a source of great strength.

You may feel inadequate to help your spouse or your other children because your pain is so great.

You may be feeling intense loneliness and isolation even when with other people.

You may feel that the magnitude of your loss separates you from others. You may feel that no one can truly understand how youfeel. The truth is they probably don't understand how you feel.

You may be dreaming about your child or feeling your child's presence nearby. You may   be searching for signs and messages for your child from the Other Side. The state of grief has an incredible high level of energy for connection to the Other Side. Messages may truly come to you because your energetic guard is down.

Important events and milestones in the lives of other children can trigger grief even years after your child's death. Significant days such as graduations, weddings, or the first day of a new school year are common triggers. At these times, you may find yourself thinking about how it used to be.

Parents are the focus of attention when a child dies and the grief of siblings is sometimes overlooked. The death of a sibling is a tremendous loss for a child – they lose a family member, a confidant, and a life-long friend. Your surviving children may misinterpret your grief as a message that they are not as valued as much as the sibling who died. You can help your children during this time of grief by spending quality time with your surviving children. Tell them that you love them. Create a safe space for them to be able to share their grief and loss. They have their own grief process. You may be surprised to hear how they experienced the loss and the time period. They are always watching and observing. Do not ever compare them to their sibling. You can say statements that edify them.

They need to know you love them. Help them articulate how they feel. This is so valuable for their healing process.

Give your children the opportunity to participate in the funeral home and graveside services. Let them come up with what goes in the casket along with you. Perhaps a hand written letter or card from them to their sibling will help. Perhaps a well-loved toy or   book could be placed in the casket by them.

Sometimes pictures of themselves are a valuable gift for the casket. Allow them to participate in the shared family grief experience. Let them help you pick the flowers. Let them write a letter to their deceased sibling that can be included inside the casket.

The siblings are often at high risk of emotional challenges as they may be feeling Survivors Guilt. Their life has changed too. They feel you by their natural intuition. They see their parents struggling to cope with all the emotional pain and changes. They may feel that you wish they had died instead of their sibling.

Warning! Pay close attention to the following information!

- Do not tell the grieving parent and family that "it was God's will for the death to happen".

- Do not tell them " Jesus needed another angel."

- Do not tell them "He is in a better place".

- Do not tell them "it is for the best".

Those are sentiments that are not needed nor wanted.

They are devastated. They are just trying to get through the next ten minutes. They are trying to remember to breathe. I cannot tell you how much I resented the people who made these comments to me when I was grieving. I resented the well-meaning folks that spoke them to me.

Parents feel alone and isolated in their grief. Friends and relatives are often at a loss as to what to say.   People usually understand grief to the level they have experienced it.

People are uncomfortable with death. They do not know what to say or how to act.

So they say stupid things or nothing at all. If you are not sure what to say--- say nothing at all.

It is better to say "I am here if you need me." Remember to hug them if they are accepting hugs.

Do not be rushed or forced into doing things by others who may be well-meaning but misinformed. Cleaning out a child's room and their belongings is very personal. Take your time and do this when YOU and your partner and/or children are ready. Some find that going through their child's belongings is a natural part of the grieving process and helps them with processing their loss. Smelling their child's clothes can bring a feeling of nearness. If you can clean out the room as a family it can help your grieving process move forward. You can share stories with each other.

Laughter and appreciation of your loved one may happen. Trust your instincts as you will know when and if the time is right.

GRIEF MATTERS!

CHAPTER NINE

PET LOSS

There is nothing like the unconditional love of a pet. They are always happy to see you. Pets are loving even when they are mad at you. Pets are beloved members of the family. Pets provide companionship, acceptance, emotional support, and unconditional love.

They are the steady in your life when you are growing up, dating, breaking up and making up. Intense grief over the loss of a pet is normal and natural. Don't let anyone tell you that it's silly, crazy, or overly sentimental to grieve!

When they die you feel a significant traumatic loss. So don't be surprised if you feel devastated by the loss of such a relationship. The intensity and longevity of the grief vary widely from person to person.

Those of us who've never established this level of connection with animals may not be able to fathom this pain. We should never underestimate the powerful draw of a bond with a being that loves us unconditionally and asks very little in return. Losing this comfort and source of joy can be incomprehensible. Losing a pet, in many ways, is not unlike losing any other loved one. It can cause feelings of loneliness, sorrow, anger and depression. We bond with our pets in different ways. How we bond affects how we mourn.

They listen to your every thought even when you do not speak. They feel you intuitively. Pets know when to come sit with you when you are sad and crying. They can tell when you are lonely or depressed. It's natural to feel devastated by feelings of grief and sadness when you're pet dies.

DISENFRANCHISED GRIEF

"Simply stated, many people (including pet owners) feel that grief over the death of a pet is not worthy of as much acknowledgment as the death of a person," researchers wrote in a 2003 article in the journal Professional Psychology: Research and Practice. "Unfortunately, this tends to inhibit people from grieving fully when a pet dies."

Coming home daily to a pet that accepts our flaws and loves us unconditionally is a source of enormous comfort and joy. Pet lovers experience the joy and sadness that owning a pet brings. Eventually we all experience the loss of a pet. For some of us, our pet is more than "just a dog", "just a cat", "just a bird", but is instead a friend and companion. For others, we may feel that our pet is an extension of the family, or we may have treated our pet like a child. Grief can be compounded when the pet was a source of comfort during certain events or tragedies, such as the death of a loved one, divorce, or times of extreme loneliness, difficulty, or unhappiness.

CHILDREN AND PET LOSS

Parents should be honest about the death of the pet. Encourage your child to express his or her feelings about the pet. Holding a small memorial service for the animal with the entire family will help children to grieve and help validate their feelings about the death of their pet. Remember that this is a child we are discussing. Children may not understand the concept of the finality of death. Television, electronic games and movies often portray the good guy dying and coming back for the next show or game.

Your child's grief is very real. Allow them to feel their feelings. Allow them the freedom of expression to grieve and cry. You can suggest they write a letter to their pet to bury with it. You can dig a burial plot in your yard and have your child be in charge of the funeral service. Let them create the way they want to bring closure for them and peace of mind. Perhaps drawing a picture of their beloved pet and putting it up in the house can be an option. Be gentle and patient with your child as they grieve. Validate their experience by honoring their feelings. Let them talk to you as often as needed to process their feelings. It is important to allow their grief process to have its time. Cry with them if you both are grieving. Hug them.

SENIORS AND PET LOSS

The loss of a pet may also be exceptionally difficult for seniors. For some seniors, their pet is their sole source of companionship on a daily basis. As a person who loves and has lost a cherished pet you deserve understanding and comfort in your time of pain. You deserve to feel acknowledged and honored as a person who is grieving a significant life loss. You deserve to feel absolutely, positively normal in loving animals as deeply as you do. You deserve to know that there is *nothing wrong* with you if you love animals as much or more than people. You have given your heart deeply and completely to another being who is now physically lost to you. You have a right to mourn. You *need* to mourn and you need support and acceptance as you do.

Your heart may be in great pain now, in pain as deeply as you have loved. Yet, there is no need to remain in pain as an on-going testament of your love. You have already proven your love for your pet probably many times over. *You are being challenged now to love not only your pet, but yourself too.* It is time now for you. Your heart is broken open now. Even in pain, your broken heart is *open.* Let love reach into your shattered heart.

There are people and animals and energies all over the universe waiting to support and nourish you. Keep your heart open and your mind open to all who are here to help you heal. We do not inhabit the earth alone. We are all here together, to love and help one another. Let yourself be loved by others. The depth of your love for your pet is a reflection of your capacity to love greatly. Let that ability to love extend to yourself now. Let that love fill your heart and every cell in your body. Even as you cry, let yourself feel the love inside you and around you. Your capacity to love and be loved did not die with

your pet. It is your pet's body that has died, not the love you share. All the love is still there. Along with the sadness, the anguish and doubts that you may ever feel joy again, the love is there. The love you and your pet share is *bigger than any pain.* It is as big as all the oceans of the earth. *Love never dies.* Feel it there along with your pain. Always be gentle, patient and loving with yourself as you heal.

<u>LOVE NEVER FAILS!</u>

CHAPTER 10

CONNECTION WITH THE OTHER SIDE

There are many mysteries of grief. One that is the most asked about is the concept of seeing or connecting with their loved ones again. Not many want the finality of grief to be true.

Most religions have a belief system about the afterlife. Christians call the afterlife Heaven. Metaphysicians call it the Other Side or Going Home.

In all the religions I have studied the question still is a very human one: *Will I get to connect with my loved one again?*

The answer is a resounding YES! Let me explain. I am just the messenger. I know we can connect with our loved ones. I have done it on many occasions.

You may hear a still small voice internally whispering a message to you. You are most likely going to be thrown about it. This is not

abnormal. You may have something

specifically symbolic cross your path. I had a friend who had a red rose grow and bloom in January in New Jersey. You may feel the Spirit of your loved one around you.

You might not see the Spirit with your eyes. You feel the love and the energy of your loved one.

You may have visits at your home or at work where items are moved from where you placed them. Items such as keys, cell phone and the like are often moved just to let you notice and pull you out of your distraction. You may feel so close in your dreams to your loved ones. They were there in your dreams. They were communicating with you. They are never going to ask you do anything that is not from the intention of love. This is a clue to discernment.

I once counseled a little boy whose father had killed his mother and then himself while the young boy was in school. Traumatized was an understatement for him. First grade

without either parent is a tough place to be.

The trauma he sustained was significant. Any concept involving trust issues was destroyed with the exception of his mother. When discussing with him his feelings about missing his mother who he had lived with he shared that she visited him every night at bedtime. I had no doubt that she had been visiting him. He could describe her and his feelings of connection with her. He shared that she stayed at the end of the bed every night telling him not to be afraid and that she loved him. She told him she would hug him when he was sleeping. That is a phenomenal experience of love and of trust.

This happens more often than you think.

Children, especially young children, have not built up the filter that we teach them to have about the Other Side. I once was at a meal with a family that was struggling to get through the death of their father and husband after the 911 attacks. This was about one year after the bombing. The three year old, who was significantly struggling with the loss of her daddy, was sitting next to me at a birthday dinner. She kept looking back into the next room. I asked her what she was looking at.

She said" Why does he not have any hands? "I asked her "who did not have hands?" and she said "my daddy". It did not occur to her that she could go visit her daddy in the other room. Perhaps she intuitively knew she could not. She did want to offer him some birthday cake though!

We need to be more like children when it comes to grief and death. Our loved ones can come through whenever they want. However, they cannot when we want them too. A talented psychic friend of mine was telling me how she spends a lot of time explaining to customers that she cannot bring their loved ones through unless they are ready to come through. They do come through if we pay attention.

Quite often their Spirits come through in the form of butterflies or dragonflies. Not always. Don't freak out if someone around you kills a dragonfly and you decide it was your favorite Uncle Bob. There exists a strong feeling you will feel intuitively that someone is visiting you. You may smell the aroma of their after shave or perfume.

My Mama has come to me in several differing forms from cardinals and blue jays to butterflies and dragonflies. She has come to visit me in my dreams singularly, along with my maternal grandmother, with my paternal grandparents and my maternal grandmother. I have gotten clear messages from her. I once was telling myself I was a motherless child even though I was in my forties. Her voice came through crystal clear and told me " that was not true and to quit being dramatic"!

My former partner suffered greatly from the horrendous and life changing sudden murder of her brother in law in Tower Two in New York City. She was so deeply affected and her grief was immense.

One late night, we were in bed sleeping, when I could feel her brother in law's presence in our room. It woke me up and I found myself double checking my thoughts. He spoke to me and said he wanted me to give his family some messages. I was overtired and grumpy and replied that she
was the one he needed to talk to not me. He told me that she could not be reached by him due to her deep grief. I got up and wrote down everything I was being told as I did not want to mess this up. He provided messages for every family member. Two things stuck out for me at this time. The first that he thanked me for nurturing his new born baby and rocking him.

This meant he was aware of what I was doing while I was at his home after he had transitioned. The second was when I told him that there was nothing that he had shared with me that the family would consider from him specifically. They were a devastated Irish Catholic family. I knew if I went to them with this information it would not go over well at first. He told me to tell his wife that "his golf game still sucks". Well, when I shared that with her she knew I had spoken with him!

Another time I was working in my healing center, in Southwest Florida, when a woman came in and just kept walking around appearing to be looking for something. I could tell from her energetic field that she was grieving. I asked her if I could help her. She said her son had died the day before and that she had hoped if she came in she could find him. She told me she was told by "her mind" to come to my store specifically. Right away, I started channeling her son through so I asked her if she would sit down so we could talk. I gave her all the messages that her son had told me. She was so relieved. He had died of an accidental overdose. He warned her through me that she had to quit drinking and that she knew this was a fact as she was an active alcoholic. He told her who should
get his dog. He repeatedly apologized for his untimely death and for his lack of telling her often enough how much he loved her. She was grateful beyond words.

There is a saying that we are but a small thin veil from the Other Side. There is no time or space there. It is not a past - present - future linear line. Actually, it feels more like it is all happening at once. Past Present Future all in time zones separate but together with each other. Think about the concept of "deja vu." A French term meaning "already seen" in this lifetime, but not in one you remember until it happens. Does it ever make you wonder how that can happen? You are going on in life minding your own business when a sudden shocking feeling hits you that you have already seen this scene play out before. It stops you in your tracks for a moment. Once you tell yourself that you must be where you are to be on your path you will learn to look forward to these events. They validate your path!

Bottom line is yes there is an afterlife. Yes, you can communicate with your loved ones sometimes. Not usually when you want however. It is not an instant gratification system here.

The fragility of your grief can open up your consciousness to connect. Stay open to thinking outside the box for messages. They are not going to write you a letter and mail it. If your loved one liked a special song it may be playing in the background one specific day like your anniversary or your birthday. You will feel the love.

Remember though that some folks are in such deep grief that our loved ones cannot get through. In that case they may come through to another mutual connection so that you get the message.

How they transitioned is irrelevant. Your spiritual and religious beliefs are irrelevant in that if they want to connect with you it will happen from their end. If you get a message be grateful! Be joyous! If you do not hear from your loved one consider opening up your mind more and learn to connect with Source Energy also known as the God of your understanding. The more that you come from loving energy the better off you will always be!

Connecting to our loved ones is one of the greatest mysteries of grief and of life!

NOTES

CHAPTER 11

FAITH

My new friend, have you learned about grief in a manner that can help you cope with it when it knocks on your door? I hope so!

One more thought that makes a great difference in floundering in the depths of grief and finding your way on your path is faith. Faith is believing in the unseen before it is seen. My research has shown that those folks who have a faith in something greater than themselves find a way to move through the grief process easier. Faith is a belief that something is going to get better no matter what crosses your path because you have a set of beliefs or tenets that support and gird you as needed. Most of those who have this faith experience have a personal relationship with a God of their Understanding.

It is not the name of the energy, but the energy itself that helps you move forward. It is believing in healing, grace and forgiveness. It is learning to live in Divine Time not Eastern Standard Time. It is learning to live life with acceptance, surrender and accountability. The Universe conspires to bring you all good when you learn to accept everything that crosses your path as a blessing and a gift. Grief matters. It can be a gift if you see it as such.

The God that I was taught about when I was a child is no longer the God of my understanding today. I can tell you that I am sure that I am loved, forgiven, encouraged, empowered and taken care of on a daily basis by the God of Love. The Universe supplies all I need through grace. The Christ Consciousness is also known as the Holy Spirit and the teachings of love that were taught by the Master Teacher Jesus. Buddha taught love. Krishna did too. So did Lao-tzu. All the great Master Teachers taught love. They also taught how to handle the pain of grief. They taught to feel your feelings and move forward. Get connected to Source Energy. I believe that all the Master Teachers were connected to Source Energy also called the Holy Spirit or Spirit. Religions have their places in our cultures. God is alive and real! Trust this Energy always. Don't buy into all the politics of religion. Buy into the Love that is real and ever present. Love is always greater than fear. Love heals all. Love helps you internally heal. Having the faith of a mustard seed will empower you. Believe it will get better because it will get better quicker when you believe it to be so.

I wish you peace, faith, health, love and healing!

BIBLIOGRAPHY

A Course in Miracles, Second Revised Edition, Set of Three Volumes, including Text, Teacher's Manual and Workbook, Foundation for Inner Peace, 1992

Fox, Emmet, *The Sermon on the Mount,* San Francisco, California, Harper San Francisco, 1989

Hay, Louise L., *You Can Heal Your Life,* Santa Monica, California; Hay House Publishers, 1982

Holmes, Ernest, *Living the Science of Mind,* Marina del Ray, California, 1984

Hooper, Richard, *Jesus, Buddha, Krishna and Lao-Tzu The Parallel Sayings,* Sanctuary Publications, 2008

Kubler-Ross, Elizabeth, *Questions and Answers on Death and Dying ,* New York, New York, Macmillan, 1974

Lao Tzu and D.C. *Tao Te Ching,* Baltimore, Maryland, Penguin Books, 1963

Mann, Janice M., *Transforming Fear and Anxiety Into Power,* St. Petersburg, Florida, Serenity Publishing House, 2012

Phipps, William E., *Death: Confronting the Reality.* Atlanta, Georgia, John Knox Press, 1987

Prabhupada, A.C. Bhaktivedanta Swami, *Bhagavad Gita*, New York, Collier Books, 1972

Webb, N.B. *Helping Bereaved Children: A Handbook for Practitioners.* New York: Guilford Press. 1993.

Wolfelt, A., *Helping children cope with grief. Bristol, PA: Accelerated Development. 1983*

Worden, J.W. *Children and grief: When a parent dies.* New York: Guilford Press. 1996

RESOURCES

ESSENTIAL OILS TO DEAL WITH GRIEF

The following essential oils can help ease you through the grieving process allowing you to move on with your life. It is important when choosing which oils you will work with to keep in mind that aromas can be associated with a particular memory and to perhaps not choose a blend that you will use in the future which could be associated with your present loss and its painful memories especially in the case of the death of a loved one.

Bergamot - Joy (Citrus Bergamia) Bergamot helps to soothe your feelings of anger, frustration and blame. It helps you see the light at the end of the tunnel. It calls forth for you to bring a sense of joy back into your life. Don't apply to skin that will be exposed to sunlight within 36 hours as it is phototoxic.

Cedarwood - Courage   (Cedrus Atlantica)
Cedarwood gives you the courage and strength to hold firm in the midst of crisis and know that you will get through this.

Chamomile Roman - Peace
(Chamaemelum Nobile)
Roman Chamomile helps you to feel at peace with the way you are feeling. It soothes your feelings of being abandoned by the one you loved.

Cinnamon - Warmth   (Cinnamon Zeylanicum)
Cinnamon helps to dispel the numbness and isolation you may be feeling. It is emotionally warming and can help you regain your passion and purpose for life.

Cypress - Transition   (Cupressus Sempervirens)
Cypress is calming at times of transition and when difficult changes need to be made. It helps you to move on in your life.

Frankincense - Calming and Centering
(Boswellia carteri)

Frankincense helps to calm and center you when your mind seems to be overwhelmed with thoughts of what must be done or should have been done. It slows and deepens your breath so you can think more clearly. It can help you break free of the past.

Geranium - Balance (Pelargonium Graveolens)
Geranium helps to even out the emotional roller-coaster you seem to be on. It brings a feeling of calm, strength, security and balance. It soothes feelings of anger, frustration and irritability.

Grapefruit - Optimism   (Citrus Paradisi)
Grapefruit helps dispel the anger, frustration, blame and depression. It brings a sense of optimism and hope for you to get through this time of loss.

Kunzea - Safety   (Kunzea Ambigua)
Kunzea helps to release the shock and pain of your loss and to know you are safe.

Lavender - **Nurturing and Forgiveness**
(Lavandula Angustafolia)
Lavender reminds you to take time to nurture yourself physically, emotionally and spiritually. It facilitates your willingness to forgive yourself for things left unsaid or undone.

Lemon – Clarity (Citrus Limonum)
Lemon helps clear your mind so that you can think clearly. It will also help uplift you mentally emotionally. Don't apply to skin that will be exposed to sunlight within 36 hours as it is phototoxic.

Linden blossom - **Love and Respect** (Tilia Vulgaris) Linden blossom brings love and oneness to your heart. It brings a respect for others and yourself.

Marjoram – Comfort (Marjoram Hortensis)
Marjoram can bring a sense of comfort. It can help stop anxious thoughts that seem to be going on in your mind on a non-stop loop. It can help you accept your loss.

Myrrh – Healing (Commiphora Molmol)
Myrrh brings a sense of inner stillness and peace that helps to ease your sorrow, grief, your feelings of loss and rejection.

Neroli – Reassurance (Citrus Aurantium var. Amara)
Neroli helps to bring a sense that things will get better. It eases emotional exhaustion and helps bring unexpressed anger and feelings of denial to the surface. It has a delicious orange aroma that uplifts moods.

Rose – Compassion (Rosa Damascena)
Rose allows you to have compassion for the situation, person or yourself and to let go with love.

Sandalwood - Stillness (Santalum Album)
Sandalwood can help you cut your ties with the past and move through your feelings of loss and isolation. It can bring a sense of clarity and moments of stillness.

Vetiver - **Grounding** (Vetiveria zizanoide)
Vetiver helps to ground you offering you
aromatic support and energetic strength
during this time of loss

Ylang Ylang - **Tranquility** (Cananga
Odorata)
Ylang Ylang helps calm feelings of anger
and frustration and brings a sense of
tranquility. Only a very little is needed as it
has a very strong aroma.

LOVE IS GREATER THAN FEAR!

DEATH IN THE BIBLE

Those of you who are studying and living a Christian life may be interested in this 18 point question study guide from Death: *Confronting the Reality* by William Phipps. It is a great opportunity to study death.

1. What did the writer of the second and third chapters of Genesis believe about the origin of death? Judging from 3:4-6 and 5:5, what meaning does death have in 2:17? Explain why the human is called "dust" (2:7; 3:19).

2. What idea found in Genesis 4:8-11 is also contained in ghost tales?

3. What strange death data are contained in Genesis 5? How does Enoch differ from the others? See Hebrew 11:5. How does the life span of the pre-flood people differ from what was stated in Genesis 6:3 and in Psalm 90:10?

4. How and why did Joseph have his father made into a mummy (Genesis 50:1-6) Compare that Egyptian practice with the customary Jewish practice described in John 19:38-41?

5. What is stated regarding the deaths of Moses and Elijah (Deut 34:1-6; Kings 2:4-14)? Do you know any songs that are based on these legends?

6. Regarding the story of Sampson's self inflicted death in Judges 16: 23-30, what case can you make that the writer thought it to be one or more of the following: a) heroic; b) cowardly; c) appropriate for the situation; d) disapproved by God; e) morally neutral. Make the same analysis for two more suicides: Saul - (I Samuel 31:1-7) and Judas (Matthew 27:1- 5).

7. Judging from 1 Samuel 28:3-20 and Deuteronomy 18:9-14, what was the general Biblical outlook on attempting

to talk to the Other Side called necromancy

8. Read Job 14:1-14 and Ecclesiastes 3:19-22 to discover the view of death contained there.

9. To what extent do you agree with the poem on time in Ecclesiastes 3:1-8?

10. In Ezekiel 37: 1-14, what is portrayed in a dramatic way? Was the prophet referring to the individuals in another realm, or to his nation Israel which had been destroyed?

11. Examine the usage of the term *hell* in Matthew 5:22-30 and try to determine its meaning. Get a definition of 7:31 and 32:35. What did Jesus say about death observances in Matthew 8:22; 23:29-31)?

12. What did Jesus say about death observances in Matthew 8:22; 23:29-31)?

13. What view of the hereafter is found in Luke 16:19-31? Did Jesus think live in a more responsible manner?

14. How did Jesus respond in Luke 20:27-38 to the question of those who were skeptical of a hereafter? Compare his reply to 1 Corinthians 2:9.

15. What is meant by life and death in John 5:24, 10:10; and 11:25-26? What does the verbal tense indicate regarding when "eternal life" begins?

16. Study, in John 20, Mary Magdalene's experience some time after Jesus' crucifixion. Do you think this was entirely a subjective phenomenon, triggered by grief over the tragic death of the man she loved?

17. What view of death and life after death
    does Paul express in Romans 6:4-11. 2
    Corinthians 4:16-5:1, and in Colossians
    #:1-3?

18. What convictions did the writer of the last
    two chapters of the Christian Bible have
    regarding death and the hereafter? How
    does Revelation 22:2 relate to Genesis
    2:9 and 3:22-23

A BUDDHIST'S PERSPECTIVE
ON GRIEVING

Written by Joan Halifax - Head Teacher -
Upaya Zen Center

The ultimate relationship we can have is
with someone who is dying. Here we are often
brought to grief, whether we know it or not.
Grief can seem like an unbearable experience.
But for those of us who have entered the
broken world of loss and sorrow, we realize
that in the fractured landscape of grief we can
find the pieces of our life that we ourselves
have forgotten. Grief may push us into the
hard question of Why? Why do I have to suffer
like this? Why can't I get over it? Why did this
one have to die? Why......... In the tangled web
of "Why", we cannot find the reasons or words
to make sense of our sadness. Dying people
also can grieve before they die. They can
grieve in anticipation of their death for all they
will

seem to lose and what they have lost by being
ill. Caregivers will grieve before those they
care for have died. They are often saddened by
the loss of freedom and options of those that
are ill and the knowledge that death will rob
them of one more relationship. Those that
have been left behind by the dying are often
broken apart by the knowledge that they
cannot bring back that which has been lost.
The irrevocability of it all often leaves them
helpless and sad. And then there is the taste of
grief in Western culture which is conditioned
to possess and not let go. We all face loss, and
perhaps can accept it as a gift, albeit for most
us, a terrible one. Maybe we can let loss work
us. To deny grief is to rob ourselves of the
heavy stones that will eventually be the ballast
for the two great accumulations of wisdom
and compassion. Grief is often not addressed
in contemporary Buddhism. Perhaps it is
looked on as a weakness of character or as a
failure of practice. But from the point of

view of this practitioner, it is a vital part of our
very human life, an experience that can open
compassion, and an important phase of
maturation, giving our lives and practice depth
and humility. To begin, it is important for us to
remember that the experience of being with
dying for many does not stop at the moment of
death. As a caregiver of a dying person or
family member who has been at the death of a
relative, we may attend the body after death
and offer our presence to the community as
they and we grieve. When the details of dying
and death are settled, then what arises from
the depths of the human heart is the many
expressions of sorrow when the presence of
loss is finally give the room to be seen and felt.
Sometimes grieving lasts not for weeks or
months but for years. Frequently the reason
why grief is not resolved is that it has not been
sufficiently attended to just after the loss of a
loved one. Family and friends of the deceased
can become consumed by the

busyness of the business that happens right after someone dies. This is one of the great problems that we face in the Western way of dying, that business is so much a part of the experience of dying and death. Survivors often face a complex situation on the material level in the after-death phase. They find themselves looking for a funeral home, letting friends and family know that a death has happened, and creating a funeral service. Unraveling health insurance, taxes, and the last will and testament also take time and energy at this stage. Later there is cleaning up, dividing and giving away the deceased's property, and other seemingly endless chores of closure.

Resorting to the business of death can be a way for survivors to avoid the depth of their own loss. Like dying, grieving has its phases, and it is important to pass through them. Similar to the phases of dying, grief can be characterized by numbness and denial, anger, great sorrow, depression, despair and confusion. Finally, there can be acceptance and even transcendence as sorrow has opened the door of appreciation and compassion. These phases are similar to those experienced in a rite of passage: separation, transition, return. Grief can also arise as a person is dying. Family and friends as well as the one who is dying can experience what is called "anticipatory grief," the bones of loss already showing. Working with that grief is an important part of what one can do in the care of the dying. In fact, most caregivers have to cross and re-cross this territory of grief in being with living and dying many times in the course of just one person dying. When my mother died, I received one of the best teachings of my life on grief. I realized that I only had one chance to grieve her. As a Buddhist, I felt I had a kind of choice. On the one hand, I could be a so-called "good Buddhist" and accept death and let go of my mother with great dignity. The other alternative was to scour my heart out with sorrow. I chose to scour. Shortly after her death, I went to the desert with photos of her and several letters she had written my father after I was born. Settling under a rocky ledge, I sunk back into shadows of sorrow. When your mother dies, so does the womb that gave birth to you. I felt that my back was uncovered as I pressed it into cold rock. Later, I was to walk the Himalayas with a friend who had recently lost his mother. The fall rains washed down the mountains and down are wet faces. In Kathmandu, lamas offered a Tibetan Xithro ceremony for her. They instructed me not to cry but to let her be undisturbed by grief. By this time, I was ready to hear their words. The experience was humbling for me. And when I finally got to the bottom of it, I found that my mother had become an ancestor. As I let her go, she became a healthy part of me. C.S. Lewis in his A Grief Observed reveals that "No one ever told me that grief

was so much like fear. I am not afraid, but the
sensation is like being afraid. The same
fluttering in the stomach, the same
restlessness, the yawning. I keep on
swallowing." Grief can call us into an
experience of raw immediacy that is often
devastating. Grieving, we can learn that
suffering is not transformed by someone
telling us how to do it. We have to do the work
ourselves. Yet a friend can bear witness and
shine light into the darkness of our suffering
and in this way help us to learn to swim in the
waters of sorrow. Ubbiri, one of the first
women Buddhists, was drowning in grief as a
result of the death of her daughter. Through
the help of the Buddha, she discovered truth
from within the experience of her own
suffering. Ubbiri came from a high family in
Savatthi. She was beautiful as a child, and
when she grew up, was given to the court of
King Pasenadi of Kosala. One day she became
pregnant by the King and gave birth to a
daughter whom she named Jiva, which means
"alive." Shortly after being born, her daughter

Jiva died. Ubbiri, terribly wounded by grief, went every day to the cremation ground and mourned her daughter. One day, when she arrived at the cremation ground, she discovered that a great crowd had gathered. The Buddha was travelling through the region, and he had paused to give teachings to local people. Ubbiri stopped for a little while to listen to the Buddha but soon left to go to the riverside and weep with despair. The Buddha, hearing her pain-filled keening, sought her out and asked why she was weeping. In agony she cried out that her daughter was dead. He then pointed to one place and another where the dead had been laid, and he said to her: Mother, you cry out "O Jiva" in the woods. Come to yourself, Ubbiri. Eighty-four thousand daughters all with the name "Jiva" Have burned in the funeral fire. For which one do you grieve? The sorrow of great and small losses is a river that runs in the underground of all of our lives. When it breaks to the surface, we might feel as though only "I" know this pain. Yet grief is a universal experience, touching caregivers, dying people and, if we look deeply, all of us. When grief overwhelms us, whether we are anticipating the loss of our own life or living with the loss of another, we can pass through the dark realms of the five elements of earth, water, fire, air, and space. We may feel forsaken as Christ was. Fearful, our body is empty and haunted, walled off from all that we have ever cared about. We can be plunged into numbness, with the very life squeezed out of us. We can drown in the cold and churning waters of sorrow or be blown like hot dry dust in a desolate landscape of depression. We can inhabit the hot exhausting dullness of mind and heart of a world without meaning, a life without purpose. We can try the patience of friends and be an embarrassment to others with our maudlin repetitiveness and self-pity. We can feel heavy with guilt or contracted in shame. We can resent the shallow and defensive reassurances that "this too will pass" or that "there is no death." Grieving is a landscape that is so varied and so vast that it can only be discovered through our own most intimate experience. It touches the one who is dying, those around a dying person, and those who survive. No one escapes her touch, nor in the end should we. The river of grief might pulse deep inside us, hidden from our view, but its presence informs our lives at every turn. It can drive us into the numbing habits of escape from suffering or bring us face to face with our own humanity. This is the very heart of Buddhism. When the 18th century Japanese Haiku master Issa lost his baby daughter, he wrote: "The dewdrop world is the dewdrop world and yet – and yet." Issa has not yet been released by the anguish of grief. But the hand is beginning to open. And like the transiency of his precious daughter's life, we hope this his grief also passed. The Zen nun Rengetsu expresses the poignancy of loss and impermanence in this way: "The impermanence of this floating world I feel over and over It is hardest to be the one left behind." Grief can ruin or mature us. Like the mother who bathed her dead baby in her breast milk, grief can remind us not to hold on too tightly as she teaches us tenderness and patience with our own suffering. An old woman once told me that wisdom and compassion are not given to us; they can only be discovered. The experience of discovery means letting go of what we know. When we move through the terrible transformation of the elements of loss and grief, we may discover the truth of the impermanence of everything in our life, and of course, of this very life itself. This is one of the most profound discoveries to be made as we engage in Buddhist practice. In this way, grief and sorrow may teach us gratitude for what we have been given, even the gift of suffering.

From her we learn to swim in the stream of universal sorrow. And in that stream, we may even find joy. For this Buddhist, this is the essence of a liberative practice.

NOTES

A BUDDHIST APPROACH TO GRIEF

by: Bodhipaksa

Grief can of course be very painful. I think the main thing I'd emphasize is that the pain of loss is very natural, and to be accepted. It's common to think that there's something wrong when we feel pain, but when our life has been deeply entangled with that of another being, the two of us are part of one emotional system — a kind of shared love that flows between us. In that kind of a relationship we're not, on an emotional level, two entirely separate beings. And so when we lose the other, it feels like a part of us has been ripped out. It feels that way because that's exactly what's happened. So take a breath, and say, "It's OK to feel this." It really is.

Even those who are enlightened feel grief.

Just as one would put out a burning refuge with water, so does the enlightened one — discerning, skillful, and wise — blow away any arisen grief, his own lamentation, longing, and sorrow, like the wind, a bit of cotton fluff. **The Sutta Nipata.**

When we think there's something wrong about feeling grief, then we add a second layer of suffering, which is often far more painful than the first. This second layer of pain comes from telling ourselves how terrible the experience is that we're having, how it shouldn't have happened, etc. Accept that it's OK to feel the initial pain of grief, and you're less likely to add that second layer.

Grief is an expression of love. Grief is how love feels when the object of our love has been taken away. And that's worth bearing in mind. Try being aware of the grief and seeing it as valuable, because it's love. Without love, there would be no grief. But without grief, there would be no love. So we have to see grief as being part of the package, so to speak.

You can treat the pain as an object of mindfulness. What we call "emotional" pain is actually located in the body. When the mind detects that something is "wrong," it sends signals into the body, activating pain receptors. The more you can be aware of where those painful feelings are located in the

179

body, the less your mind will have an opportunity to add that second layer of suffering.

You can recognize that a part of you is suffering, and send it loving messages. While you're paying mindful attention to the part of you that's suffering (noticing where in the body your pain is located) you can say things like "It's OK. I know it hurts, but I'm here for you." You can find your own form of words if you want.

Lastly, it's worth reminding yourself that all living beings are of the nature to die. It's a natural part of life. We don't do this to numb the pain or to make it go away, but to help put things in perspective. Today, thousands of people are mourning the loss of pets, parents, even children. You're not alone…

The enlightened feel grief, but it passes for them more quickly than it does for us, because they recognize that everything is impermanent, and they don't add that   second layer of suffering.

So your grief is natural, but I hope it soon becomes easier and easier to bear

SUICIDE ISSUES WORKSHEET

Here is a question and answer worksheet to investigate this complex topic of pain.

Answer yes or no for each question. Jot down your opinions and thoughts on a separate piece of paper. Then go back and take a look at your thoughts after some study time. See if any of your thoughts have changed. If you have had a loved one who has committed suicide take time to write down your thoughts about suicide prior to your loved ones loss. Then look at your thoughts now. Have they changed?

1. Is suicide a sign of insanity?

2. Is suicide a sign of being overwhelmed emotionally?

3. Is suicide a selfish act?

4. Do you think that you could have stopped your loved one from killing themselves if

you were present when it happened?

5. Is suicide a reactive action?

6. Is suicide a premeditated act?

7. Is there a moral difference between suicide to escape a miserable life and suicide to escape a miserable death?

8. Should terminally ill people be assisted in suicide if requested?

9. Do alcoholics commit suicide more than sober people? commit suicide more than non-drug addicts?

10. Do those who commit suicide have to be in pain?

11. Do those who commit suicide go to Purgatory Hell? Heaven?

12. Can someone with a beautiful heart and soul commit suicide?

13. Can you pray for their soul after they are

gone? Does that help you or them?

14. Can you forgive the person who commits suicide?

15. Can you believe that their suicide was part of their life path? Why or why not?

16. Can you access your anger about a suicide?

17. Can you access your woundedness about a suicide?

18. Does repeatedly asking "why?" help you?

19. Can you access your frustration that the loved one who committed suicide didn't reach out to you first?

Made in the USA
Middletown, DE
13 November 2017